Understandin'
Better
By and By

By Thelma Craig

Dedications

I would like to dedicate this creative memoir to my granddaughters, Addy and Madi. I hope that they will be forever blessed with the knowledge, wisdom and grace from God and the Women that He place in their lives. I have hope that they will cherish the lessons and strive to become great women of God. Oh, and I want to uplift my grandsons, Marcus and Ziggy- May they be blessed with knowing, loving and ultimately respecting powerful women in their lives. Additionally, I would like to dedicate this book to my Mama (Thelma, now deceased) and my Great Grandma (Jenny Lee, now deceased) and all the mothers who came before them.

I acknowledge my Husband, Jeffrey Craig for his undying support and encouragement. Also, I would like to thank all my friends who believe in me as I believe in them. Because I truly believe that iron sharpens iron. I must admit, I have made many attempts to publish this book. Therefore, I would like to thank Rudy Brown of Stupendous Copy for consultation and Ifalade TaShia Asanti for editorial support. Most importantly, I thank God for all blessings.

Table of Contents

Introduction

Understandin' By and By is a book about me and a book about you. As the hit song by Chaka Kahn says, "I'm every woman. It's all in me," this book reveals the womanness in all women, and the gifts we give each other. This book also tells the story of indispensable women who have positively impacted my life. Through these stories, it is my hope that you too will be positively transformed.

There were experiences in my life growing up where I was programmed to doubt myself. These experiences also created a feeling of unworthiness within me. In my book, _Understandin' Better By and By_, I share the process of my undoing this programming and guide readers to recognize where and when they might've learned to doubt themselves.

I have two granddaughters. They are beautiful, bright and blessed. They have strong-willed countenance. They are aware and assertive. They are opinionated-even the one year old doesn't take any stuff. This is in part because of how their parents are raising them and what I as their grandmother am teaching them. They call me their, "Nana" which is a cultural colloquialism used in the place of Grandmother. As their Nana, I see their personality and their spirit. As I watch them grow up, I recognize how important it is to pass along positive reinforcements using words, gestures and feelings. I regularly affirm who they are as girls and share with them ways to become great women.

I also share with them how wonderful it is to be a woman. I teach and guide them with ease. I understand that is up to their parents to teach them balance and give them what they need to be healthy and productive.

In the meantime, I recognize the legacy given to me by my parents. They taught me how to survive, serve and thrive. And through those lessons, I developed a relationship with myself and with God. Through those relationships I became conscious and awakened. I also recognize that all the experiences I've gone through helped me become the person I am today.

As a child, naturally some of my experiences made me feel vulnerable and afraid. For many years, I dwelled on those experiences some of which felt like an attack. I also discovered a thread that led to a trail of survival. This thread was interwoven with a series of lessons. In this book, I reflect on those lessons and share the pearls of wisdom I have gained from them.

One of the lessons is my recognition that people are placed in your life for a reason. The people we encounter are all pieces of the puzzle that makes up who we are and what we become. When I sit still and reflect, I see the people who taught me the greatest lessons as angels and messengers of God. Even when I feel lonely, I can see how I wasn't and never am alone. Because God always sent people to support me when I most needed them.

Some of the people that God sent helped to shape and mold me. Because of how their presence in my life impacted me, I say they were a Godsend. God sent them to me even when I was unaware. We are sometimes unaware of the blessings God brings to our lives through His messengers and angels.

The book *Understandin'Better By and By,* helps us learn to stay in the moment. It also teaches us to recognize the gifts and the lessons that that God brings us. I believe God gives us signs when He is teaching us something. How do we recognize those signs? How do we recognize the angels that that carry the banner and deliver the messages God wants to bring to our life?

The Holy bible--which is considered God's Word--mentions signs from God. The bible says, "We will know the signs." So again, how do we stay in the awareness and recognize the signs that God gives us to show we are on the path He created? How do we know when to respond the call, heed the lessons and receive the gifts God continues to bring?
The first step is to recognize when we are being taught and primed. This is where our legacy begins to unfold. The legacy I inherited from the women who showed up and out in my life gave me a reason to like myself. I knew they had experiences that shaped them as well.

Many of the women I encountered could be classified as strong women. I have my own interpretation of what a strong woman acts like. What I can tell you is that these women passed something along to me that supported me in my journey of learning to love God, myself and others.

Chapter 1
Grace

A week before the funeral, my sister talked to me about her vision for my mom's homegoing celebration program. She started the conversation by saying, "I talked to my friends who plan funerals for a living."

My sister supports her friends and church members by ushering at funerals in the Community. She goes to funerals to show love and caregiving. She also consoles many grieving families. That is to be admired. She knows all the matters of the descendants, the mourners and their families. She is capable of standing in the gap for them. I always admire this quality in women. In the old days, they called people like her community Sisters.

Two days before my Mama's funeral she said in her way of asking but telling you what to do. "I want us both to speak at Mama's funeral."

Never in a million years did I think I would have to stand next to my mom's coffin and speak about her. I've always imagined and lived in fear and thoughts of being unconscious as a result of the pain and agony I would be in. I thought if she died before me, I was going to react dramatically. I stuttered a bit when I responded. "I-I-I...I'm not the one," I said. Her request made me remember that I have attended funerals since I had the capacity to remember. I remember being 8 or 9 years old going at my first funeral. Her asking me to speak made me think about my past experiences. It was always a family member. My Mama's cousin had the most impact on me. I just didn't like to attend them.

I used to always feel so small when she presented and made requests of me in those early childhood times. I now know it has something to do with the big Sister- little sister syndrome. I felt intimidated. I thank God I don't feel that way anymore. I guess I'm more confident in myself now. She meant well. But I was always a little bothered when she gave me her infamous look that said, "This is what you must do, Mama would want you to do this... This is what you need to do for our mama". It was the look and the tone always bothered me and made me feel like the little sister. She was gentle yet demanding. But I know she was just being the big sister. This was not a bad intention. It really was a humble request. Maybe that's what did it. I knew that I had to show up for or mama. Maybe this was lesson for my growth. I just had difficulty with the prospect someone telling me what to do. I felt like, Hey I'm am a grown woman now. But we never grow up in the eyes of our older sisters.

We tend to make assumptions when we are hurting. My mama just died, and I was feeling all kinds of things. I ignored that recurring angst and took a deep breath. This time I had talked to my mentor before I went there. Her advice was to breathe. So, I breathed, and I pondered for a few minutes and then consented. I chose to take care of mama and speak at her funeral.

Then, my Sister then gave me a look of gratitude.

During the week of making funeral arrangements I thought hard about a theme for my Mom's homegoing celebration. Now that I had committed to speak on the special and emotional occasion. Frequently, I thought about changing my mind. Thank God I had a hard time going against my word. So, I took more deep breaths.

Then I knew what to say…. I was going to talk about my Mother's relationship with God. Well, bits and pieces of it and what I experienced it to be. I rationalized that she would want me to tell the world that she loved GOD. And she did. She had a huge relationship with God. Since God was at the center of her life, I need to tell the world about what a mighty mama and a woman of God she was.

I thought about her dedication to the Church. I thought about how I perceived her walk with God. How she sent us to Sunday school every Sunday. Sunday school, Main Worship Service, Prayer Meeting on Wednesday nights—we did it all. All at her guidance and instruction. We had to go to church. I thought about her service in the Church. How she sang in the choir. She had made us serve too. I was on the Youth Usher Board. Before I realized it, I was having a good time. I enjoyed being on the youth usher board. In fact, I loved it! It gave me a sense of pride and joy. Now I understand it. I see what mama was guiding me to.

Later, I realized that my destiny and purpose was to assist and serve. When I lifted others up, I was lifted up. We don't realize it when we are going through the mama process or being raised. My Mama was raising me to be a Woman of God. My Mama was guiding me to my purpose. Being on the usher Board, my love in serving is now apparent that those were signs and experiences from God letting me now know that I was on the right path.

Back to the funeral and my talk.

I usually got upset with my mama when she made us walk to church. When we had to walk to church it usually meant one of us kids had been acting out, resisting the Sunday ritual. But when Church service started, I was seated in the Usher Board pew. I remember one particular church service where my Mother sung a solo. She sang a song called, *Grace*. The lyrics to the song still stand out. "God's grace is sufficient for me." I can hear her singing like it was yesterday.

I remember thinking, *"But Mama can't sing!"* I listened to her sing with closed eyes and seemingly an open heart. I was mesmerized and embarrassed at the time. But I realize today that she could really sing. I guess it was just strange for me hearing my mother croon.

Just like my Mother finding the courage to sing that day, I knew talking at her funeral was part of my assignment and my growth. I had to have courage. I had to have strength, ammunition and power. The Word of God. I googled the lyrics to the gospel song, Grace. There were just as many renditions of the song as there were artists who had sung it. Little did I know that her singing that song would be forever embedded it in my heart.

I also looked up the scripture in the bible that referred to Grace. I remembered it being in 2nd Corinthians. In this scripture, Paul says, "But he said to me, My grace is sufficient for you, for my power is made perfect in weakness". (NIV)

I studied and thought about that scripture until it was time for the funeral. I can honestly say that I was terrified of standing up to speak alongside my mama's coffin with her in it. But I did it. And I wasn't crying. In fact, I was calm. But looking back I think I might've had an out of body experience. It would take years for me to remember everything I said that day.

I stood up, walked over to Mama's coffin and took a deep breath. She looked more peaceful and beautiful than I'd ever seen her. We had dressed her in a pink silk suit, pink hat, white gloves in a dustpan mauve coffin. Mama had picked her coffin out four months earlier. I had admonished her to get her affairs in order.

Later, the funeral director shared with me how mama sat in her office, eyes closed, only to open them slightly and pick out a coffin. She had stated where she wanted to be buried with a peaceful expression and resolve on her face.

During the service, I remember looking out over the church. Even though I could see no faces of the hundreds in attendance I said, "My name is Thelma. Mama named me Thelma after her. Over the years, I frequently asked her, "Why did you name me Thelma?" I did not like that name. Her response would always be, "You will understand in the by and by." Of course, that always frustrated me.

When I was standing there next to her I realized, this was the by and by mama had always talked about!

I continued my speech.

"Can't you see the way I hold my hands, the way I put my hands on my hips, the way I act, talk and dress? I now see the many attributes I share with my mama. Y'all know what I'm talkin' 'bout? Look at me now. It's the by and by ya'll.

I continued, "Mama taught me about intuition, faith and trust. I have learned that they all work together in my relationship with God. I witnessed her crying a lot during my childhood. I wondered why if she had faith and trusted in God, why was she crying. I now understand she had faith and trusted god immensely.

I remember when she made us walk to church because my siblings and I were misbehaving all morning. I think she just wanted us to walk so that she could get dressed and ready for church in peace and quiet. On that day, she had a solo to sing in the choir. She needed peace to prepare for her performance. Walking to church, I was so embarrassed and upset with mama. Many church members passed us along the way and asked if we wanted a ride to church. But we knew mama would not like that because another reason she wanted us to walk was so we would think about our behavior.

We managed to get to Sunday school on time. The Youth Usher Board gathered for a few minutes before the service started.

   We were all dressed in our white blouses and black skirts. Our knees were vaselined. Our hair hot-combed. We wore white gloves. We were ready. Church started. Mama was in the choir pew with her newly pressed robe and wig of the week. She was looking good as usual. That was her trademark-- looking good. Her neighbor stood up during the expressions part of the wake and said, "I couldn't wait until Sunday morning, so see Mrs. Thelma walk out of her house every Sunday like clockwork, dressed for Church, matching hat, dress, shoes and purse " She was a fashion lady always something to see. She said she stood outside until mama passed her house and waved.

   Back to my story. They went through the pre-worship, the call and response, then the piano played. When Mama stood up my heart dropped. I said to myself, "Oh noooo. Mama can't sing."
I covered my face and scooted down in the Usher Board pew way in the back. The pianist played the first stanza then I heard my mama's voice. My eyes opened from behind my hands, as I peered through my fingers and realized her eyes were closed too!

   Grace. Grace. God's Grace, is sufficient for me.................
People started clapping and tapping their feet. This went on for a while because typically, when the soloist gets happy, the choir and the pianist start hammering

the song out over and over beyond the limits. They play until they make their point.

I continued. "My Mama taught me about Grace in the repetitious sense. She kept falling down and she kept getting up. She lived her life in the church and on her knees in prayer".

While I was planning her funeral, the word *grace* stayed on my heart because of that memory. So, I googled, "God's Grace" in the bible. The first scripture that came up on the screen was what Paul had said in 2 Corinthians, Chapter 12, verse 9- which says, "My Grace is sufficient for you and my power is made perfect." (NIV)

When I had quoted the scripture at Mama's going home celebration, I referenced the incorrect scripture. I referenced and stated 2 Colossians. I remember a voice throat cleared, "Uhm Uh", I looked over at a Sister Deaconess who was also my mama's friend. She cleared her throat loudly, stared at me sweetly and mouthed the correct name of the verse which was 2nd Corinthians. I stood corrected and got back on track with the eulogy.

I explained what Grace meant for my mama.

"My mother had struggled, cried and battled three cancer surgeries. In her brain and colon. But she kept going. Just like how Paul described in 2nd Corinthians 9:12, "Therefore I will boast all the more gladly about my weaknesses, so that Christ's power may rest on me. (NIV)

I stood in the front of the Church and testified to my Mama's faith and how it was GRACE that sustained her and how GRACE was my testimony. Truth be told, I was preaching and delivering a sermon at my Mama's funeral. That was one of the most influential experiences in my growth and transformation. Never did I think I would be standing near the pulpit of the church with Mama resting on the side of me in a beautiful pink coffin. I had always imagined myself fainting or crying uncontrollably if my Mama died. But instead I exhibited courage and grace. That's what I shared with the folks gathered. My sermon was about everything my Mama taught me. And I wanted to testify about it.

Chapter 2
Mama - Her Namesake

Mama used to say, "God may not come when you want him, but he sho do come on time."

It was fortuitous when one of her friends stood in the gap at my mama's wake and said the words that she always said. And I am a witness to mama's truth. Because one of my current challenges has to do with impatience. That's what I'm working on with God's help. I am learning to wait on the Lord like Mama used to talk about.

Today, I can see how patient and accepting my Mother was. I didn't realize during those childish challenging moments of my youth. I thought she was mean. But my childhood friends loved being around my mother when I brought them home. They thought she was nice and very funny. I noticed the same characteristics in me when I became a parent. My kid's friends enjoyed coming to our home and I loved when my kids invited their friends to our home. I do wonder sometimes if my kids thought I was mean. I also wondered if I like my mother, was impatient and accepting and if I greeted my child's friends with warmth and understanding? Maybe even a little fun loving.

Back to mama…My Mama was a fighter. At her funeral, my Uncle, her brother, told a story about how she had become a fighter. I had never heard this story before. He shared about the time when he and Mama used to walk home from school. A group of bullies from school had started following and harassing them. The bullies terrorized them and made them run home daily. Until one day my mama's mother told them to stop running and fight back. The next day, when the bullies came after her and her brother, she beat them to a pulp. So much so, my grandmother had to admonish her for fighting. But it was too late. A fighter was born. She never stopped fighting and protecting her brother. She never stopped fighting in life. As I look back, I realized Mama was humorous, kind and sweet in the presence of my friends and peers. But with me and her other children, she was that fighter. I used to wonder, does she like my friends better that she likes me? Kids always think that their parents are different with others. I know now that Mama was just being Mama. She was real and authentic. She knew no other way to be. She was always in survival mode. You have to be real to survive. My mama was a "tough love" mama.

My mama endured a lot. She worried about her bills. She worried about how to make financial ends meet on her maid's salary with child support from my Daddy. She worried about being separated and ultimately divorced. She worried about when and if people talked about her. When she worried about the money she included in her tithes and offerings to the church offering table. Most of the time it was just an offering because the tithe would take more than she could afford. I realize now that she was teaching me a crucial element of survival. To give and serve even in your hard times.

Mama had other struggles that made her worry. Later in life when she learned that her new man had cheated and produced kids. I didn't know all the details about her second husband's indiscretions, but I remember asking her how she could continue in a relationship that I thought should be broken? "Sometimes you have to let go and give it to God." She said, "he can't help what he did. He didn't mean no harm". She said she forgave him.

She followed up with another memorable line. "That's how he was raised."

She always took her pain to God. She prayed constantly. I heard her cry in prayer after work. She would come home, make sure our chores were done, retreat to her room cry and pray. I saw her jump and shouting praises in church as she left it all on God's altar. She was thanking and praising God like there was no end. Sometimes Mama's jubilation embarrassed me a little. But thankfully she usually stayed in one spot. Mama wasn't one to dance around the church. She was mindful of the large feathered wide brim hat she wore and her new, carefully chosen outfit. So, those hats t never left her head during the most fervent praise times.

I get it now. Mama was grateful and filled with the Holy Spirit. She found relief in glorifying God despite the challenges she faced. She was jubilant because God's grace had come right on time on numerous occasions. I learned how to give God praise even during challenging times by watching my mama. I also learned that God's grace is always right on time.

Mama was also a dreamer. She really had prophetic dreams. I used to hear her tell her friends the details of a dream from the night before over the phone. Days later, I would hear her confirming what she dreamed had indeed manifested. Mama's gift with dreams was passed onto me. Mama believed that you had to have good health to receive clear messages in the dreams. By good health she meant having a healthy gut. Because she believed the gut was where your intuition was housed. I remember her saying if you get a funny feeling in your stomach, pay attention because God is trying to tell you something. Ironically, Mama did not take always take care of her own gut. This might be part of the reason she died from stomach cancer. And I realize it was challenging maintaining a health gut diet on her salary and eating history.

Mama did take care of herself in other ways. One of the ways she exhibited self-care was not taking no stuff from people. She didn't hesitate to let people know how she felt when she was wronged. She was always good with them after she got it off her chest. With us, I used to think she was just being mean, but now I realize she was giving us tough love. When my friends came by to visit, I envied the laughter, the jokes and banter between them. I wanted her to make jokes and be funny with me all the time. Now I understand she had to be firm while raising us. She had to be stern with us. She felt alone.

Four months before she died, I visited her in a hospital in Florida where she lived. I wasn't clear on what she in the hospital for. She led us to believe the doctors weren't clear on what was wrong with her. But today I wonder if maybe she didn't want to scare me. It seemed like the hospital staff was being intentionally vague. It was either that or they were incompetent in how they communicated with her family. This is one area I wished I had been more diligent. My Mama's health care. We should ask more questions of our health care providers.

I learned a lesson about being proactive in your health care. I also learned that sometimes you have to support others in navigating America's complicated healthcare systems. Mama thought she'd had what she called a mini stroke—whatever that means and that she had meningitis. But she was vague about her prognosis and treatment. I know now it was incorrect. I needed to dig deeper to get a full understanding of her condition.

Mama was delirious by the time I got to her. She was unconscious when I walked in after a long flight. But after I got there, she started to move around. The nurse said this was the first time she had showed signs of life. The fact that my presence impacted her so positively made me happy. Mama moved her mouth, hands and then her head. After a few hours in my presence, she started to mumble, then talk and just say things from the top of her head. Random rumblings and hallucinations. She said this…. She said that. Then she let out a loud roar of laughter. She laughed and laughed and laughed. She flung her hands and arms around. She laughed so hard until she cried. She began to cry and cry and cry.

My mother had to be tough. She was a single mom. I didn't realize that she carried the tough label until the day she died. I mean the very day she died. Mama had been through so much illness, afflictions, heartaches, disappointments and endured so much pain. Yet she always got up and kept going. She had a brain tumor, colon cancer, stroke, high blood pressure. You name it she had it. By God's Grace she got up and kept going like that infamous moving "Eveready battery". She lived and thrived 82 years trusting in God.

For as long as I can remember, I lived with the fear of my mother dying and leaving me. I walked around with that anxiety. She surprised us all by dying before her last husband, George. And my Daddy who was her first husband. It was sad watching my Daddy go up to her coffin at the wake. My husband later told me that he heard my Daddy say, "I didn't think you would go before me." He too thought she'd outlive him. He died exactly six months to the day later.

Later, I would remember him whipping out one of his favorite handkerchiefs as a tear dropped while saying goodbye to my Mama. As always, Mama refused to be predictable. She couldn't let her either one of her husbands' beat her in going to meet the Lord. But she let go. As I look back, I realize my mother was a little competitive. I'm not sure if I inherited her competitive spirit. Maybe it shows up in other ways. I beginning to understand it now.

My mama had a powerful sense of fashion. Her philosophy was, "looking good and feeling good go hand in hand." Fashion made her happy. Growing up,

24

she taught me that what you wore really said something about who you are. I too like clothes, jewelry, hats, shoes and purses. But if I can't have an item, I let it go. She was a great seamstress and often supplemented her income with making clothes for other women. Our home was full of Simplicity patterns, fabrics and all kinds if sewing paraphernalia. She was an expert. I also see now that this was her relief from stress. The sound of the sewing machine was her music. I know now it was mine too. When she was sewing, she was relaxed, peaceful, not worrying, not doubting, but being faithful. It was a great time for us, because she focused on her time sewing.

I like to coordinate the clothes I wear. I like to match sometimes and other times I like to take a different route- funk it up a bit. I might mix plaids with a paisley type of fabric. She also knew how to accessorize. She would make or buy a dress and then go to Rheinurs (a Nordstrom's today) and purchase the most beautiful accents, on sale of course. I now combine stripes with flowers whether it be the shoes or the skirt. Mama enhanced my freedom to be creative with fashion. Mama was a seamstress and eventually became a tailor. People used to say that her creations did not look "Mammie made". She also designed without patterns. She excelled in her craft. That's how she mastered the art of adorning herself and dressing her children with the best fashions.

Mama taught me to show up as my beautiful self and to always wear my garments with a glorious attitude. There is a scripture that captures Mama's philosophy on fashion and appearance. It is Isaiah 61:10 which says, "I will rejoice greatly in the Lord. My soul will exult in my God. For He has clothed me with garments of salvation." I understand this now. "He has wrapped me with a robe of righteousness, as a bridegroom decks himself with a garland and as a bride adorns herself with her jewels". That's why I buried Mama in high fashion.

One of my most powerful examples of courage and grace took place while Mama was in the hospital the last time. I'd had a serious talk with her about getting a home health nurse to help meet some of her needs. I'd also talked to her about making sure her affairs were in order. I had surprised myself by confronting her about such matters. Even though I feared that I would eventually lose her, I had to do it.

Mama never fully recovered from the illness that had hospitalized her that last hospital stay. The doctor called me to say that her cancer was too advanced and there was nothing he could do. He said she had about six months to live and that she was being transferred to a hospice facility.

I asked the Doctor to wait until I got there before telling Mama the news about her impending death. Somehow, I felt she already knew. I immediately booked a flight to Florida. I found a ticket for $93.00! I was blessed to find an inexpensive flight with such a short window of travel time. I only had one layover in North Carolina.

While waiting to board the flight the I paid attention to everything and everyone. It was like I was having an out of body experience which I assume was my inner response to the news that Mama was dying. With only ten minutes to board the flight, I realized my boarding gate had changed! Somehow, I was able to get to the correct gate on time. The very same thing happened with my second flight. I was saved again by Grace.

The night before my flight, my sister had kept me posted on Mama's status. She gave me the address to the hospice, and she said she was concerned about being transferred before I arrived. I asked them to wait, I asked them not to take her to hospice until I arrived to escort her. They did not wait. They claimed the needed the hospital bed.

My Sister told me that Mama kept asking, "When is Sista coming? What time will she be here?" That was all she talked about was me getting there. She was said to be peculiarly anxious about my arrival.

As usual, my stomach was topsy turvy from flying. Only this time it was more intense. I rented a car and was on my way to the hospice when it dawned on me, I hadn't eaten anything. I wanted to stop for breakfast but that still small voice inside said, "Continue on the journey to see your mama." It felt urgent so I followed the guidance and kept driving. I sensed she was waiting anxiously. I arrived at a pretty building surrounded by orange groves. The scent of the oranges was beautifully intoxicating. It brought back all my childhood memories of traveling through the groves with my mama as a kid. Before entering her room, I took a deep breath and noticed the number on the door was #7. My stomach jolted and I knew God was up to something. I thought I had six months, at Least that's what the Doctor said.

When I walked in and my mama laid her eyes on me. It felt intense. God was getting ready to do something in her, I thought. She smiled a wide grin and said. "You made it! You made it. My baby made it."

I kissed her on the cheek and smiled. My mama took a deep breath, closed her eyes and immediately went into unconsciousness. The nurses were in and out checking her vital signs. They were always smiling. My mother did not regain consciousness. Friends and family members came by throughout the evening. I stayed with her until late into the night. To my surprise, a childhood friend (who I mentioned earlier in the book) who'd lost her parents when we were kids stopped by to sit with me. We talked and laughed throughout the evening until I left to check in to a nearby hotel.

Surprisingly, I had a peaceful sleep. Early morning, I walked into my mother's room and noticed her shallow breath. The nurse informed me that her breathing was deep, and she thought it was her time. I panicked and tried to call my sister and my niece. Anybody, I called. No one was able to get there at in time.

The nurse placed her hand on my shoulder gently and said, "Talk to your mama, she can hear you. I put my big girl panties on, held my mother's hand and began my prose. I told her everything I ever thought I wanted to say.

I recall saying, "Thank you Mama. You did the best you could. I know It was tough. Thank you teaching me to look both ways before crossing the street. Thank you for teaching me how to look inside. Thank you for telling me about God and faith. Thank you for being you." I was surprised at the things I had to say to my mama.

I know we shared this encounter, this connection for a good fifteen minutes. My Mother's hand moved like she heard me.

I finally said, "Mama, you know how you always talked about being in the presence of the Lord? Well go on mama, He's here waiting for you to come to him." In that very instance, my mother took her last breath! It was so amazing. I could not believe she took that breath when I spoke those words. A great peace came over me. I was happy and sad at the same time. This was one of the greatest gifts of my life.

The fear was gone. My mama taught me so much about life in her death. And the words that she spoke while she was alive will forever be my guide.

My hand in yours, yours hands in mine
God held our hearts
No questions why,
*I stood in the gap for you to pass me by...**thelma craig***

29

Chapter 3
My Great Grandmama- My Sage

My Uncle, the family historian, said that my Great Grandmother died at the age 103. I believe it. She was elderly in the royal sense but was still vibrant and sharp throughout her entire life. She died on December 25, 1982.

My Great Grandmama facilitated the journey and migration for some of my mother's people and father's people from Georgia to Florida. I often wondered why they migrated to the south. This was an exodus for these families. They were sharecroppers under tense conditions. It was escape.

Great Grandmama was from a place around Bainbridge, Georgia. My Daddy told me that the house she was born in was a "lean too" on the property. I plan to travel there again. It's sad that we don't always value our family history or persist with further questioning of our elders while they are still alive. There were many missed opportunities to attain the information that would support a sense of pride in knowing who and where my people came from. I hope this book serves as a reminder to share information with our children and grandchildren and that we encourage them to learn more about their family history.

I was interested in my family's history, but I did not persist. I heard what they said but should've been better about recording what I heard. Things like Great Grandmama saying often that she had, "Indian in her."

That fascinated me. She had beautiful long black hair cascading down her back which she kept plaited and tied in a head wrap. She also had powerful high cheek bones and strong beautiful legs. Her shin was the color of coffee before the milk. I do recall wanting to drink coffee when I visited her but Great Grandmama would say, "Coffee is too strong for your little soul."

My Great Grandmama was a mystic and leader in her own right. She gave us all nicknames. She gave my brother the obvious nickname, "Brother." She also taught my brother to fight for his sisters and to speak up and tell the truth about whatever situation he found himself in. She always admonished him to look her in the eyes, tell the truth and be proud to accept the consequences if he did something wrong.

My brother was a true brother. He died at the early age of 22. After his funeral, I saw the first and only tear from my great grandma's eyes. He had a special place in her heart. She loved and admired us. Today I realize and appreciate the role he played in my life. Even now, I miss the protection that my brother gave and represented. He also taught me how to fight the bullies in my life. He once said, if you don't fight back, when you get home, I will fight you and beat your butt! After that, I fought those bullies and won. The bullies didn't bother me again.

Great Grandmama dubbed me, "Sista." It sounds like it's written. That name was so branded in me, that some hometown people to this day don't know my birth name. Even my peers didn't call me my given name. They called me Sista or my last name. My siblings, cousins, aunts and uncles also called me Sista. Still today, they call me Sista. She also called my Aunt CeCe Sista as well.

Great Grandmama called me Sista because she saw peacemaker qualities in me. The Sister, the friend, the go-to girl. She cultivated that. When my siblings fought, she looked to me to intervene, even thought I was the youngest. There were other Sister personalities among my relatives who also exhibited the helper, peacemaker spirit. But Great Grandmama expected me to be the strongest in for making and keeping peace among them while demanding the baby sister attention and respect I deserved. She also taught them to protect and fight for my siblings while teaching me to value and treasure their protection. She said I was everybody's Sister. When my mama and Daddy brought me home from the hospital, I was told that my siblings asked "Who is that? She said, "That's your Sister and she is Sista"

She wore a black felt or straw hat, carried a knife in her knotted stockings and slept with a gun on her nightstand. Her bed was on the side of the window and close to the door which meant she would be among the first to respond to intruders. She dared us to touch the gun but also explained how it was dangerous for us kids to fool around with her gun. Needless to say, we never touched her gun or her knife.

Great Grandmama was my Daddy's mothers' mama. She loved herself some Daddy. I thought he was her favorite because he was the only one to move close to her when settling with his family. And she did not apologize for her preference. She encouraged Daddy to move his family to Ocala Florida where she had settled and built her home brick by brick. He was in contact with her each day. That would be my birthplace. My other siblings were born in the everglades of Florida. Daddy took great care of her and she watched out for him. All his siblings cared for her and she cared for them as they visited often.

Great Grandmama had connections with some powerful and prominent white men in Ocala. She used those connections to help her children. Great Grandmama knew her grandson (my Daddy) was a wild one, as she called him. Let's just say, Daddy stayed at the top of her prayer list. He always said, "If it wasn't for Grandma I wouldn't be here'.

Daddy would stop by her house every day during and after work. She was instrumental in getting him the pharmacy delivery job at the famous Andrews Walgreens drug store. The drug store was prominent in the town because many wealthy white retirees migrated there. Great grandma had a connection to Mr. Andrews, a wealthy White man in the town who owned the pharmacy. She also did laundry in her home. They brought the laundry to her for washing and ironing. She was my first known entrepreneur. We lived close to her home so that made it easy for her to keep her eyes on all of us. We lived walking distance. When my mother worked, she was our caregiver. Great Grandmama built her house by saving and acquiring the cider blocks every month. I really meant it when I said the house was built brick by brick.

I used to see her tie money, coins and banknotes in a handkerchief and fold it carefully to tie a knot at the end and place it in her bosom. That was her savings account.

She would look at you as you watched her, smile and tuck the money away under her sagging breasts then carefully button her blouse or dress. Winked her eye and laughed. She did not wear a bra. She was always hot and said that underwear confined her. Made her feel wrapped too tight. I now realize I have the same aggravation. I can't stand to sleep in underwear. I don't feel free. Like I'm wrapped too tight to sleep. If I'm wrapped too tight, it makes me have "worried dreams," just like Great Grandmama. She sat on her front porch with the church fan, lifted her dress and fanned herself regularly. The Florida sun was hot!

Great Grandmama had a true Florida, Geechee accent. She said things like "yesddiddy" (yesterday) and "fo day" in da morn (morning time after midnight). Or "gwine" , that meant going. She was also a dreamer and a Sage who spoke often about her dreams to me. Her dreams were vivid, prophetic and blessed with important messages. She also saw the ancestors.

This entire book could've been about her. Maybe that will be book two. But for now, I just want to write about the rich and beautiful things she taught me about being a woman and her impact on me. Great Grandmama made me feel proud of who I was. She instilled in me the knowledge of the power that I had. She told me I was beautiful. She scolded me when I cried because kids had called me black and ugly. She was one of the women in my life that pushed me, encouraged me, believed in me and blessed me. She held onto every word I said—she knew my gestures, my eye and hand movements. She openly admired what I was dressed in, no matter the occasion. Whether it was playtime, school or church time, I would have to stand in front of her while she sat in that old blue rocker and twirl. Twirl so she could she the way the hems were placed at the bottom of the skirt. Twirl so she could get a good look at how the collar around my blouse was constructed. She was in awe. She just laughed and ooh and ahhhhhhed. I could see the reflection of her smile at my black patent leather shoes. Even though she and mama didn't always see eye to eye she gave mama her props. She would say, "Yo mama sho can sew".

She knew my mother made and considered very carefully what we wore. She made sure we girls had pressed hair, that my brother's hair was cut and that our ears were clean. She always expressed pride and admiration in everything about us, especially how we showed up on her front porch. This is how appreciating fashion became a part of my spirit. Now I love the design of a garment. I value the fabric, the colors and the cut of an outfit. I take pride in how I present and show up in the world. I now twirl in the mirror for myself, thanks to her.

Great Grandmama was a force in my life so powerful, that now when I dream, I can see myself respond or act in Jenny Lee fashion. After I have had a powerful dream. I ask, "How would Great Grandmama interpret this? Then I realize she would encourage me to see and figure it out myself. I got the important messages from Great Grandmama in my dreams after her passing. She came to me in one particular dream that I deeply cherish. She pointed toward two tall trees. They were Georgia pines that grew immensely in the Florida national forest area. Georgia pines loomed incredibly high creating a picture across the central Florida sky. She pointed and gestured, "Sista, see those owls up yonder?." Perched on the specific trees, two owls on each tree which were adorned with jewels and glittery tapestry.

She asked again, "Do you see the Owl on that tree?

I asked, "The little one?"

She said, "No fool, the big one. That is the one for you." ("fool "or "foolish" was an endearing term she used – I understand that now)

I looked at the big beautiful big owl draped in jewels and my mouth opened in awe.

"You mean the big one is for me?"
The big owl initially facing away gracefully turned her head toward us and stared into my eyes. She looked at me with a powerful knowing. Her big ol' owl eyes were wide and aqua. The layers of jewelry glistened in the dusty evening. I felt as though I was looking at magic. My Great Grandma smiled. She was truly great.

Jenny Lee was an outspoken woman. And oftentimes used profanity. She had no shame in that. It flowed from her tough like syrup. It was like she did not care what others thought about her. Yet the entire community respected her. However, she was the "Mother of the Church". The word I heard her say most often was "shit".

"You shitting me! Or, "Shiiiiiit."
When surprised or amazed, she said, "No shit?" When something was told to her she could not believe it. She would say the word just before she is laughing out loud. "Shit, shit, shit." Or, "You shitting me." You full of shit". Lawd, He got foolish eyes".

Now, don't Judge,,,,, it was not profane when she used it. It did not diminish who she was to me or the folks around her. She commanded and received respect. I understand it now. She did not abuse the word to attack others.

Like Mama, my Great Grandmama, also taught me about the importance of a healthy digestive system. When I was a little girl, I would hold my bowels. I held it because I could not understand why that stench, smelly substance had to come from me. Because of holding it, I would frequently experience constipation. In her exasperation about me holding my bowels, my mama would take me to my Great Grandma's house to perform the old-fashioned hot water bottle enema on me. She had no fear or shame about doing this. I was embarrassed and ashamed. Yet, she assured me that this experience is nothing to be ashamed of. She attended to me like it was her only purpose in life. Like she was there to relieve me of my concerns, pain and distress. She would laugh and say, "You got to let that shit go, baby Sista." Her garden consisted of green onions, Vidalia onions, rutabaga, cabbage, leeks, collard and mustard greens. All the ingredients for a healthy gut. She was careful about what she ate. My Great Grandmother was intuitive and believed the gut area was where we carried wisdom. Jenny Lee was also a dreamer, a sage and a wise woman. She was not what you'd expect a grandma to be in the prim and proper sense of the word. After all, her favorite word was SHIT. She was actually quite comical because when she said the word shit, because she always said it with a smirk and a wink in her eye. So, when I had to go to her to be relieved of shit, I felt loved.

I can say I knew her well. But there are many missing parts to her story that I would like to discover. I was once told as told that she was married six times. I used to ask and think how can you love that many times? My Aunt told me that Great grandma did not believe in divorces. So, this could just be a story. I don't know how the alleged marriages ended or began. She had one daughter, my paternal Grandmother. My grandmother married a Murph, so did my great grandmama. But the last sir name she used was Brown.

Great Grandmama had a mischievous sense of humor about her life experiences. Especially all the relationships with men. Myths and stories of her life abound. My Aunt once told me that Grandma use to say, "I went with a married man so long, I fell in love with his wife." She had a powerful sense of humor so this could be a joke. She went to Church and prayed to

Jesus, though she was not self-righteous. She also wasn't judgmental.

Great Grandmama was the Mother of the Baptist Church we were raised in. The Preacher of the Church would come to her to get approval about his upcoming sermon before preaching it. If she approved, the sermon was presented and blessed.

She would always sit between the two huge pecan trees in her backyard and instruct us as we picked the already dropped ready pecans around the tree. After picking we would deliver the pecans to her waiting apron on her lap. First, she would approve or disapprove the collection and add only the good ones to the pile in the bucket by her feet. We thought we were doing the most important task of our lives. We were proud to bring her the fruits of our labor and she rewarded us with a wink.

Great Grandmama survived the challenges of her day and age. She also made it through the days and years despite the pains of the work, the men and the storms she weathered in living 103 years. She was a stocky, big hipped, big legged, big boned beautiful black woman. Her skin was dark brown bronze. Her hair was very long, way past her shoulders. It was black with gray strips dominating as far back as I can remember. She used to love it when we all sit on the porch together. She would sing, "Hey Sista, Brother or Mooch. Go and get my hair fixings from the front room. Get my brush, comb and hair oil." The front bedroom was the place she held sacred. No one could enter the room without permission. She did allow my aunt CeCe to sleep in there once when she visited. She had a cedar chifforobe, mahogany bed complete with laced pillows and bed coverings. Her silver brush comb and mirror were a pride and joy. I remember polishing them on occasion.

Then she would ask me, my sister or my brother to comb her hair and scratch her scalp. My sister and I fought for the chance each time. She just smiled and told us to get to it, even if you both must do it. She let her hair down from the long braid and relaxed. I recall now how ceremonious that felt to me. Combing her hair soothed her. This was her selfcare. Her hair glistened and draped down her back. She would close her eyes. That did not mean she wasn't aware of us or what was going on around her. I could see her entire body just let go and melt into her old rustic blue wicker rocking chair. That chair had cushions handmade by her from old scraps of fabric from a worn dress. Even though they didn't like each other, my mother would send Great Grandmama scraps of fabric from her sewing. She used those scraps to make things like the pillows, cushions for the chair and quilts. I wish I had those quilts today.

I guess you could say Mama and Great Grandmama had an understanding. This is how I learned that you don't have to see eye to eye with everybody. You can love and respect another woman in your life despite your differences.

The kids in my family always hung out with Great Grandmama on the front porch. She like to watch the people pass by. And they all knew to respectfully acknowledge her. I continued to comb then brushed her hair for about ten minutes. Then I plaited it and applied the balm on her scalp. She sat with her eyes closed smiling and enjoying being cared for. Oftentimes, she would say how good it felt. Those were very sweet days.

Great Grandma admonished me and always told me to stop crying when the other kids called me black. She said, " Shit!, fool ,don't you know , the blacker the berry the sweeter the juice" . She said I was the prettiest black girl she ever did see. Oh, mention again that she loved to use the word "fool" or foolish when she reprimanded or scolded.

My Daddy once showed me the lean-to house Great grandma was born in. We traveled from Atlanta, through the Bainbridge area on our way home to Florida. My Daddy pulled off a lonely dusty dirt road to a place outside of Macon, Georgia. He said, "see that old leaning place, that's where grandma was born and raised". He knew I was always immensely interested in hearing stories about her. I was always in awe of her so much that I was almost paralyzed and could not stop asking questions. I imprinted that scene in my mind and spirit. It was said that Great Grandmama was a pistol. Maybe because everybody knew she carried one and would use it. When we stayed overnight with her, she laid that pistol with a long frame on the nightstand next to her bed. Below her old brass bed was a little cot. Two of us had to sleep on the cot together. The other would sleep in the bed with Great Grandma. It was an honor and privilege to sleep with

41

her. But you had to be quiet. This was her prayer time. She would position us along the side of the cot. All four of us would kneel, bow our heads and clasp our hands. She would commence to praying. It always sounded like a song. Her song prayer started with "LAWD, LAWD, me and these here chillen is bowed down on bending knees …….. Thank you LAWD GOD……..."

She had the best quilts on that bed. I loved the fact that Great Grandmama lived in a house that she built. As cold as it got sometimes, I felt safe when I slept with Great Grandmama. Sometimes it was drafty. I'm talking about a bone-chilling cold because the house had no drywall. The house was made only of bare cinder blocks, but the bricks were painted of course. When I slept on the cot, I always wet the bed. Yes, I was bed wetter. Grandma did not get angry with me because of the wet bed. It was like she knew why and knew about my fears, thoughts and concerns. She knew that I was sensitive and was experiencing things in my mind that I could not comprehend. She also knew I was a worrier. She said so.

She used to say, "stop worrying or you are just too full of shit, letting people get on the inside of you. She said, "you don't have to be "fraid" of nothing or nobody. Grandma is here. Just trust in the LAWD- you are his chile". This is how I now know that trusting in God was key. Not to worry. My gift from her. She knew that I felt everything. She knew that I worried about my family and the people in my environment. I was an empath.

I recall the time I came home from College. She was so proud of me. I was the first to go to college in my immediate family. She sent me five dollars during my first month at college. She made me promise to call her when it came in the mail. She said the other students might try to steal it, take it out of the mail. She was a cautious, warning grandma. She admonished. Her five dollars was a million to me.

When I came home after my first year in college, I went to her house. She was sitting in front of the potbelly stove poking the fire. I sat in another rocking chair next to her in Her chair. *You never sat in grandmas chair.* Her seat was in front of the stove, just a little angle off to the side so she could poke the fire, add a log and watch the flames glow and shimmer. She was the only one allowed to stir and poke her fires. She settled down in this cozy moment to talk to me, She said "Sista, I seent you flyin."

I sat with my mouth wide open like I was wondering what she meant and how to ask her to elaborate. I think I knew. I knew that she was telling me that I was experiencing and discovering things about my gifts and myself. I sensed that she knew I was learning in school because I was the first to go to college in my family. She believed and trusted that I would pay attention in class and absorb all I could. She was our constant teacher about getting things done, completing chores and developing discernment which she called, "studying on things." She was always talking about discernment. Because she knew I was far from home for the first time and needed to keep my

43

intuition on point. So, I recall, she didn't seem to worry. It was as if she knew I was going to be alright. She was certain that I would be taken care of. There were times she shared her precise wisdom with me. "I have something to tell you, about you, about me." I was so innocent, wide eyed and impatient, imploring her to talk faster. She just looked at me and said, "You are not ready yet." I regret not being mature enough to sit and listen when she wanted me to be still. That is precisely why, even in her afterlife, I speak to her when I have a most powerful dream. I often wish she could still interpret for me. But in my soul, I know and hear her telling me to figure it out. You got this. You're the big owl now. Still building my confidence, even now.

When I think of my Great Grandmama and the impression she left on me, my heart swells and I want to sing the famous song by Aretha Franklin, "You make me feel like a natural woman." My Great Grandmama was powerfully natural. She paid special attention to what she ate, what she wore and what she said. She paid attention to people's intention and their mannerisms.

She watched and observed me like a hawk or like an owl. She expected respect and she got it. She had sharp intense eyes. When she wanted something, she didn't have to ask for it, it was just intrinsic. And that is what I experienced with her. She walked what she talked.

I do not know what her height was. I just remember that she walked powerfully tall. She could have been five foot three inches. Yet her presence and her aura were tall. And she is why I know I must stand and walk in my power. The power that God gave me to be the natural woman that is my inheritance.

She was our go-to babysitter, our shelter in the storm. When my mother found a part-time maid's job, while my Daddy worked full time, we had a home at grandmas. It was truly a second home. I felt more at home there than anywhere.

My Great Grandmama was truly great. She stood in her power. She was respected by the community leaders, both the Colored and the White leaders.

My Daddy adored her. He said, "If it wasn't for grandma's prayers I would not have survived as long as I did." Just like my Daddy, Great Grandmama made me proud to be my authentic self. My Great Grandmama made you feel like wherever you are, that was the place to be. If you were in Georgia, that's it. If I was in Florida, that was it. If I am in Colorado that is the place to be.

Through her, I learned that wherever I am, I stand in my power. I imagine what she endured as a sharecropper living with her family in Georgia. When she moved our families to Florida, it was an exodus. They had survived and endured. She settled and thrived. She was powerful wherever she was and that is my lesson. Home is wherever I am with God and the people I love.

Great Grandmama also taught me about my gifts of the spirit. She taught me that I need to be patient. I can see now that I am still learning how I am showing up today.

I got my gifts
I see their cause
I got my clothes and my twirl
I have to wait, hope, create
*I must obediently pause….***thelma craig**

Chapter 4
Aunt CeCe – Elegance

My Daddy's older Sister was the most beautiful woman I had ever seen. Breathtakingly beautiful. I always stared at her when she came to visit from the big city Philadelphia. She was one that left during the great migration. Her and hers went "up north" for a better life. Apparently, she made it to the promised land because when she returned home to Great Grandmama's house she looked rich, sophisticated and successful. Of course, at my age, I saw her beauty inside and out, not just her external appearance. She was not on the planet very long during my lifetime. I was very young when I stared and gazed upon her. She spoke with a Northern accent which was very noticeable among us Southerners. Her hair and clothes were stylish and impeccable. She wore white gloves on an ordinary day! She always gave me the most assuring smile. And she would say, "Sista, you're beautiful too." How did she know what I was thinking? Did she see the admiration in my eyes? Was she put on my path by God to give me a glimpse of, "I am beautiful too"? Was I given her for such a small span of time so she could have the most powerful effect and impression on me?

I skipped away to join the other kids playing outside, feeling oh so satisfied. I think she knew that she was giving me a message that would carry me through the tough times of feeling ugly and unworthy. She was born in Florida and I remember her traveling back for visits to the family home on the Bryant Plantation in the Everglades. I also remember her coming to Ocala to see my great grandmother where I felt safe.

My Great Grandmama really adored this granddaughter. She allowed her to sleep in the front bedroom! The one room in the house you could not enter without her permission. The front bedroom in her house held her finest chests, a chifforobe doilies covered dressers, quilts and fine linen. The chifforobe held her best dresses inside and her hats on top in special floral hat boxes. I always adored the silver mirror and hairbrushes that were placed ever so special on the dresser. I knew this woman; my aunt was special to her when she stepped out of that room to greet us. During the regular days staying with and visiting great grandma, you had to have special permission to go in that room. Aunt Cece was tall (at least seemed tall to me) lean, cocoa dark, with slick straight hair that curled flipped at the ends. She had pearly white teeth. She smelled like a rose. Her smile reminded me of my Daddy. She was his big sister and he loved the ground she walked on. I was very young when she died but I remember the redness and puffiness of my Daddy's eyes at the time of her death. My love for her intensified because he loved her so. I don't ever think I saw him shed another tear during his lifetime.

My Aunt Cece was in my life a very short period of time yet she had a great impact on my little soul. She gave me the beautiful image of the woman that I was meant to become. That I could relate and was really related too. We had the same blood! Her smile, the sway in her walk, her laugh, the way she said my name, were all beautiful attributes. I like to think that I too show up like that for young girls who are doubting their beauty.

Beauty on my mind
Beauty on my heart
Because of you, I see it with my eyes
*In my Spirit....***thelma craig**

Chapter 5
Miss Susie-Mysterious Womaness

Miss Susie had a baby. His name was tiny Tim. She put him in the bathtub to see if he could swim. I remember that childhood nursery rhyme or playtime tune as one we Black kids knew so well. As God choreographed my life, he intentionally placed Miss Susie as a neighbor to the right of my childhood home. Miss Rotham (I will tell you about her in the chapter ahead) was the neighbor on my left. Two opposite women, different in every way.

Miss Susie was our mysterious and mystifying, next door neighbor growing up. I had a sense that she was different in a powerfully enigmatic way. I was drawn to her. Mama seemed leery about her. And everyone else seemed to talk in hushed tones when they mentioned her name. She perplexed me. In a way, that always watched her. We could see into her house from the back door and the carport of our house. Our houses were close, but we had a very distinct boundary. We had a fence between us. Miss Susie seemed was a beautiful woman. Her skin was dark, almost blue black. Her teeth were pearly white even though she dipped CC's Snuff. She always kept her hair pulled back from her face in a ponytail. She wore floral dresses around the yard and home. When she went fishing, she wore cache pants and a simple button up blouse with black high-topped water wader boots. She fished a lot. I always pondered how uncomfortable they must have been in their car with several bamboo fishing pole hanging out of the window from the inside of the car. I guess Miss Susie waded in the water. Oh, how she must have admired water. I got that sense that she did. I now understand that Miss Susie was a natural woman and valued nature. I always saw a birch stick hanging from her mouth. They called Miss Susie a "root" woman. Well if it meant she worked with herbs from the earth. Yes, she did.

One day, Miss Susie brought home a man. His name was Tim! Yes, just like the Ole nursery rhyme. He was a very handsome and a very young man. He seemed much younger than her. That's not to say she was elderly. The young man was tidy and neat. He was cordial and quiet. He did not look directly at me. Even at my young, age I knew he was a beautiful man. But he seemed like he could pass for the age of someone that could be her son. He was her man. He was tall and slender with dark curly hair that matched his mustache. He was a gentleman as far as I could tell. We would all wave, as he returned the greeting, he kept on looking straight ahead. You would never really know because Miss Susie kept him under lock and key. She watched his every move. We called him Mr. Susie. He didn't mind (of course we didn't say that to his face). He was always smiling. I could see that he was happy man. I could tell from afar that he loved himself some Miss Susie. He didn't seem to have chains on him, like I overheard the people gossip about them. They used to always say she worked a spell on him. I didn't know what that meant. I still don't. Maybe this is one of those things I will understand better by and by. Just maybe she just gave him love that was meant for him. She engaged him in the chores in and outside of the house. He would mow the lawn, repair the fences, plant the garden and trim the trees. Weekly, like clockwork, I would see him as he hung laundry on the wood stand wire clothesline, leaving their clothes and linens out to dry in that hot sunny Florida weather. I could see from my yard that he took in the laundry and folded it in the wicker baskets. He was a neat and meticulous man. I'm not sure if Miss Susie was as tidy and meticulous as her man. She was always seen lounging in the backyard under the shade tree, as he carried on with the chores. I know that she cooked. I could smell the aroma from our carport through her side house window. She was a lady of leisure though. I didn't know if she had a job. I mean a leave-the-house-go-to-work-job. I noticed they would always come back with the car loaded with outdoor equipment and long bamboo fishing poles hanging out the side window. I would see Miss Susie unpack the fishing gear and fish from the car. Buckets, poles, ice chest and baskets. She looked pleased. I was pleased because I felt that she was having fun. I wanted to go fishing with them.

Everybody did not like Miss Susie, but I did. She was the object of gossip in the community. They thought her strange. They judged and wondered about the young man she had living with her. They wondered why she didn't socialize with them. She was doing no harm to anyone as far as I could see, and as my mom testified too one day. I can testify that I never saw her disrespect or treat people mean. From what I saw from my carport, backyard and bedroom, as I was always was in awe of her because of her mysterious being, she was wonderful. She was mysterious, unusual, evasive and surprising. The neighbors whispered about her. She and my mom had a neighborly cordiality about them. They spoke, nodded and acknowledged each other every now and then. They would talk over the fence. My mom would often initiate the conversation when she was under the carport closest to Miss Susie's' side of the house.

My Mom would say without looking directly at her, "How do Miss Susie?"

"Fine, how you Thelma?"
The niceties would go on for a few minutes.

I remember a time when, Miss Susie said, "I'm watching your house, don't you worry none."

Mom smiled and went about her business. They had an unspoken friendship. An acknowledgment that means, I am your true neighbor and friend. And, I don't have to be in your face, and you don't have to be in mine. I got your back. They respected each other. My mom minded her business as a neighbor and so did Miss Susie. They did not need to socialize to know that they were neighbors and on the lookout for each other.

One time I saw Miss Susie sprinkling a yellow substance around the edges of her entire yard. My mom and I were peering out of the window. I asked my Mom what that was and why was she doing it. My Mom said it was sulfur. Later, I saw my mom do the same thing. I think it was to keep the snakes out of your yard. Maybe real and metaphoric snakes.

Miss Susie also burned sage from time to time. Her house would be lit from candles in the evening starting at dusk. She would sit out at night under the moon with a small barn like fire. I saw her making oils and soap form her back porch. The aromas coming from her house varied from day to day.

What did this mysterious beautiful Black woman teach me? She taught me about being a mystic. And it was intriguing. This beautiful spirit taught me that it is ok to burn sage, light candles and to pray. She was a witness to me that it was ok to have a lover treat you like a queen, to wait on you hand and foot and to love you. She also taught me that it is lovely to mind your own business. And not to care much when people gossiped about you. She let me know that if people don't like you, it's alright. Do you, be you. Live your life within your life and seek explore the good mysteries of life. And finally, she taught me that there was nothing wrong with learning about the elements and majestic God made powers like the moon, the stars and fire. There was something interesting in exploring all the mysteries in the world that a woman who has mystery knows.

Your mystery is sound,
Mystic Angel was bold,
Blow your horn in my heart,
*Honor and grace abound….****thelma craig***

Chapter 6
Miss Rotham – Sophistication

Miss Rotham lived next door, on the right of our house. She was a woman who exemplified loving kindness. She had never married and to my knowledge had no children. She was a proud Deaconess, Methodist Church lady and was very prim and proper. While writing this book, I researched her and discovered that her walk as a Deacon was part of her ministry to guide and support others, especially women.

Like me, she had a desire to lead a ministry to empower women. That's why God put her on my path—to recognize the gift that was bestowed upon her and to recognize that same gift was bestowed upon of me.

Miss Rothams' home was always manicured to perfection. She had hired an elderly gentleman to come by and take care of her yard. I think Miss Rotham was sweet on him. She always made sure she was home when he came to do the yard. I watched her do little things to let him know he was special. She'd be outside serving him cold water, iced tea or lemonade. She didn't ask my brother or the other boys in the neighborhood to attend her yard. It was always this genteel man who smiled while he worked. I wouldn't have been surprised to have found out she was "sneaking" around with him, in a sweet capacity of course. I sensed a powerful connection between them. Miss Rotham was very discreet, and I respected her privacy. I just watched them from afar and took note of how Miss Rotham treated her secret helper.

On first Sundays, Miss Rotham wore a white dress and fancy handkerchief on her head. She always got dressed earlier than we did so I was able to witness her as she prepared and presented herself for Church. I saw the carefully dressed woman take pride in what she wore for Sunday communion. Other Sundays, she wore a conservative, button-up dress with a thin patent leather belt both to highlight her beauty and conceal the imperfections on her waistline. She wore pill boxed hats with a net attached halfway over her face. Subtle lipstick. She was graceful. Miss Rotham was a looker with her caramel brown skin and pleasantly plump body. I could see her clearly because her front door faced our side windows.

I usually watched her from my bedroom window while preparing for the late service. I could see all that was going on at Miss Rotham's home. She was a pleasure to watch. Her short, stout stature exuded power and fanciness. She was the kind of woman that made you stand or sit up straight when she gave you a side look. You instinctively remember not to slouch and quickly spit the chewing gum out of your mouth. The quality of this woman influenced my soul and made me recognize the same power she had existed in me. She commanded respect and proper social proclivities

People gossiped about Miss Rotham, too. Yet they kinda feared her. They said she was a snob. If I knew then what I know now, I would've told the talkers that yes, Miss Rotham does have an air of superiority.

Not in a sense that she disrespected others but that she was confident in her own knowledge and taste. She knew how she wanted to show up in the world and she did it in her best way. I really appreciate God for putting this lady on my path.

Teatime was Miss Rotham's most gracious time. She had all manner of fancy tea sets in her china cabinets. I would linger a bit too long while surveying her house when she called me over to give me a bible booklet or magazine. Miss Rotham invited a few ladies over once a week to sip tea and chat. I perched by our living room window to hear them talk and see her greet them with the brightest smile. I got a kick out the blue and gray hairstyles they wore. See!, dyeing the hair blue was in then. I watched her welcome her guests as they arrived with the lalala chatter.

"How nice to see you."

"You look lovely."

They sounded like the chattering birds that circled our homes. The laughter and spirit that came from her house was almost magical. I think Miss Rotham knew I was watching because she would glance in my direction and smile. Her smile told me this was her finest hour. Her tea guests were all fabulous in my eyes.

Today, I enjoy gathering sister friends for warm tea and sharing our femininity. I got a glimpse of my own creative whimsical self from the moments of peering into Miss Rotham world. That was how the sociality of teatime was embedded in my soul.

Having a high tea also marked another important event in my own life. On my 48th birthday, I finally accepted the loss of my brother who had passed away 27 years prior. I decided to celebrate his homegoing with a High Tea at my home. I celebrated my birthday while honoring the blessing of my brother. That was when I finally let go of the grief, I experienced for so many years after his death. The tea was amazing. I asked all 25 women to come and bring a memory or celebration of a woman who inspired them in their life to share with the ladies. It was awe inspiring. We cried and we laughed, we loved on each other and we had tea. I felt the spirit of Miss Rotham and my brother there. I also knew she was placed in my life to inspire me to experience and revel in the art of celebration.

Miss Rotham also kept a bird. A parakeet. Later, this memory would inspire me to have a bird in my college apartment (the efficiency, midtown Atlanta). It was just the two of us. His name was "Baho", which meant, "Full of Joy."

Reading was another gift Miss Rotham gave me. I used to gaze at Miss Rollins while she sat in her living room in a fancy rocking chair reading a book. I could hear her old grandfather's clock chime every hour. Later, I would long for a grandfathers' clock and ended up purchasing one for our first home. I had to have that beautiful sound of time in my home. Our major purchase with the home.

Miss Rotham made it her mission to give us bible story children's books from the church just in case we weren't getting the proper message in our Baptist affiliation. She gave me my first copy and subscription of *The Daily Word*. This publication provided me with scriptures and stories that I could relate daily life to.

Miss Rotham was a proud Church lady. You could tell she was gregarious in her youth. Her gray hair was styled neatly around her head like a crown. Her home was a reflection of the way she dressed and carried herself. Crystal candy dishes filled with assorted sweets. I'm reminded of orange slice jellied candies rare find today. She offered you a piece each time you bought her mail or newspaper from the driveway. Makes you want to stop and appreciate the simple things in life. This is what will heal us. Just remember.

There were starched doilies adorning the chairs and tables. The bushes in her yard were always filled with colorful and aromatic blossoms. I once watched her cut lush flowers from a bush. I watched her clip them, bring the bouquet to her nose, close her eyes and sigh. Because of her affinity for being surrounded by beauty, I strive to appreciate the delicacies and niceties around my home. I beautify my environment and embrace the peace and harmony I create.

I now understand what this woman gave to my life. Miss Rotham gave me a view of being prissy without the prudishness, formal with softness and to express generosity with grace. Those are the qualities I would later develop and come to love in myself.

A touch of dainty here
Brushing my spirit with softness there

Letting go of the rough edges
*Touching into loving kindness…***thelma craig**

Chapter 7
Mendy -Found My Voice

My first-grade school year was an enormous reveal. I made my first real friend—her name was Mendy. She was the middle child of twelve siblings. She must have felt powerless in the scheme of them all. Whew! Mendy was something else. She seemed powerful to me. Mendy excelled at all the games little girls played at that time. *Jack Stones, Tic Tac Toe* and *Dodge Ball*. She was also assertive and a bit of a bully. She was powerful, fun, bossy and confident. Maybe I like her for her aggressiveness. This was a confidence I was lacking. Along with the things I liked about her, there were some things I would later reflect on that were lessons I'd never forget.

Mendy was my first best friend or so I thought. She was popular but not necessarily smart. She was competitive but not clever. She was forceful, dominant and confident but she was also that bully that knew how to bait you and keep you on the hook. I was in awe of the way she bossed everybody around. The boys liked her, the girls feared her. I revered her.

Mendy had the nerve to tell me not to wear certain new outfits my Mom made or bought for me. My mama would call me in the house to try on a dress she'd just made. Mendy was over to play and witnessed me getting this present. I still remember the bright colors, the paisley print fabric with just the right frills, lace and hemline. When Mendy saw the new outfit my mother presented to me her head fell. She would cringe and roll her eyes at me and at the gift. She would sulk and our play turned unfriendly. When we were out of the presence of my mother, I recall her saying, "That is not a nice dress. Don't wear it to school." I didn't understand, but she was adamant. "You better not wear that to school tomorrow! Or I will beat you up". I surrendered. I must say here that a year or so later, my brother taught me how to fight bullies. He taught me how to fight back. And win.

I always felt a sense of wonder and confusion at how Mendy could boss and bully me and other kids at school and get away with it. There were times she would take all of my lunch money because I wore something new. She was supposed to be my friend— my best friend. I thought maybe that's what friends do.

I just wanted a friend I could trust. Someone to share my secrets with, support my dreams and desires, encourage me and allow me to encourage her or him. I wanted someone to support me when all the other kids teased me and called me the black ugly names. Mendy didn't want to share or protect, she wanted to take things from me. Taking my coins, fruit, my cookies were among the things and demands she put on me. Today I realize she did like me but was also jealous of me. Jealousy can create barriers for making true friends. You can't harbor jealousy or envy and truly like or love a person. I became to understand this by and by.

I enjoyed being in Mendy's company except for the times she was making fun of my apparent weaknesses. She told me what to do, what not to say and made me bring her something from my house to prove I was grateful to be her friend. This is where I had to learn boundaries. This is where I had to learn to take pride in myself and not let others push me around. I liked my friend Mendy but I did not feel respected by her. I realized that she was asking me to stand in the shadow of her instead of standing in the light together.

What did this woman, girl, peer, childhood experience teach me? She taught me how to recognize abuse. I learned that I was made to be a friend to people but before I could be a friend to someone, I had to be a friend to myself. Respect my self, love myself. I began to understand in the by and by. I value friendships now. But I quickly and can discern when people in my life are toxic and are not for me. I understand how to be a friend.

I've had experiences in life where I had to remind myself of the experiences with Mendy. Particularly when I am approaching new and potential friendships. I have learned to nurture and maintain the best of my God given friends. My mama used to say all the time, "If you have one good friend you are blessed. If you have two, you are lucky."

I learned that I cannot be controlled by another person's projections on me. That lesson hit me hard when I realized Mendy was a bully. My brother told me the same thing several times, but I wasn't ready to listen. Mendy did not want my light to shine. That was the beginning of my lesson in learning not to give anybody the power to snuff out my light.

I was also learning discernment and to recognize when people are for me. I learned how to appreciate a person for who they are but not lose myself in that person. I would experience other people like Mendy later in life until I became a woman who would not let anybody bully her. Friends should add and bring value to your life. My first friend Mendy added value but she also took value away from me.

Our friends are here to show us the connection with and projection in each other. When a relationship has a positive impact on us that positivity will show up in the next relationships we have. My first friendship with Mendy taught me to value my own power and to know when I am standing next to another powerful woman. Iron sharpens iron.

Little hearts open,
Small souls present
Taking in all that we know
*Sweet understanding broken….**thelma craig***

Chapter 8
Grandma Honey, Her Majesty

I remember when I had my first experience with the flim flam. As struggling college student, I was on my last five dollars. I was standing in line at the bank when I was approached by an African woman who appeared to be lost and desperate. She offered me a deal. Little did she know I only had $2.32 cents in my account and $2.68 in my pocket. Long story made short, I ended this scenario by jumping out of a moving car on Peachtree Street in Atlanta, Georgia.

As irony (or synchronicity) would have it, my maternal grandmother was being scammed around the same time. I remember the call from my mother when she informed me, "Yo' grandma was flim-flammed." That's when I realized I had gone through a similar experience. In my flim flam, the other person got flammed and I, once again, was saved by God's grace.

They called my Grandma Catherine, Miss Honey, Aunt Honey, Honey Honey. All sweet names—but I never thought of her as sweet. She was might and stern. Miss Honey appeared at my Mom's bedside the day before she was scheduled for colon cancer surgery. Did I mention that my Mom was like the Eveready battery? She had illness after illness, but she kept on going by the grace of God.

Miss Honey sat quietly next to my Mother. Their relationship had blossomed and healed. They had intense love for each other. In the past, there had been an unspoken something that kept them at odds. I felt the same energy between them when I was a child. Whatever it was, it had kept them from fully expressing their love for each other. The lesson I learned from them was to take the time to heal the wounds and misunderstandings with women who are special in your life. Your daughter, mother, aunties and true friends. Doing this will help support your transformation and healing. It will also strengthen your relationship with God.

I walked into the hospital room and said, "Hey Grandma."

She nodded. Grandma never showed too much emotion.

She said, "Sista, you look good. Your skin, your eyes. Your hair is coming in just like mine." She was referring to the halo of gray at my temples around the top of my head. She removed her hair bonnet and smiled. The gray was around the edges of her head like a halo too. I had never connected this attribute of her to myself. So this is where I got my crown. It was her. Her majesty, her stamina and her queendom.

I had always thought she was a mean grandmama. She was tough in discipline, no nonsense and spoke straightforward to the point when I saw her. She did not have a lot of words, but she used her expressions to communicate. When she gave you a look, you instinctively knew what she meant. Sit down, be quiet, you should be seen and not heard. I knew the expression that communicated whatever she was saying. I was a little afraid of her even though she was not physically abusive. She never gave us spankings. She just relied on the "look" to express her disapproval or pleasure with whatever you were doing. I learned to keep her good eye on me by being obedient and attentive to her expressions.

Grandmama Catherine liked her Folgers coffee strong, black and hot. I used to sneak and taste that dark syrup on an occasion and regretted it ever since. Grandmama's spirit was strong just like her coffee. Her presence was power, even her cooking and household management took the lead strict position.

My Daddy used to say, "Miss Honey don't play." He followed that statement with a story. He said, "I have never been afraid of her though. She respected me and I respected her. Even when yo' mama and I had disagreements, Miss Honey said ya'll had better straighten it out, work it out but you better not hurt my daughter. Somehow, I think she knew your mama was the one to be feared in the fight. She knew that her daughter often started the fight and could very well finish it. She was not that worried about me hurting yo' mama."

Thinking about Daddy's story made me remember the time my mama packed us up and fled to Riviera Beach to her Grandma and granddaddy's home. I always felt welcome by her husband, my Granddaddy Buster. But Grandmama, she was not the essence of her nickname, Honey. Sometimes she wasn't so sweet in my little opinion. But that was my misperception.

It was a Christmas time. My Grandmama seemed annoyed when we arrived on her doorstep. The tree was up. The plastic Santa was on the door. Poinsettias were displayed around the house. She decorated the house wholeheartedly. She was a staunch Christian Woman.

I wonder if my Grandma's love for Poinsettias are the reason I love them so?

Grandmama's house was supposed to be a refuge. It should've felt like a warm end to a long ride down to southern Florida. I did not feel comforted. I felt like my grandma did not want us there. It was like she was disappointed by my Mama leaving and not staying to fight. Looking back, I realize she didn't know how to show emotions. She did want her daughter and her kids to feel safe. I understand it now.

I was so excited when my eyes saw the Christmas tree in Grandmama's living room surrounded by gifts. Everyone sat down around the tree.

All the gifts had someone's name on them. Except for me and my siblings. Our names were not included.

My Grandmama was one who took in her children's children. But it felt like we were not included in the list of children she took in. I think she had expectations that my mama would care for her own children.

Grandmama had always taken care of the grandkids that were left at her doorstep. She did it like it was her purpose. She carried the weight of that responsibility with her like it was a part of her body. The home was always full of grandkids.

I got the feeling that since she and my Mama had this thing between them, she didn't want to help her and her kids. She felt like she had taught Mama how to take care of her own kids and she should know what to do. She had those expectations of my mama.

My mama was the oldest of seven children. I thought that Grandma not getting presents for me and my siblings was her way of saying to my Mama, "You are strong. You don't need my help." My Mama was just taking a break from my Daddy. She had intentions of going home. In Grandmama's mind, because she always liked him, she felt that my Daddy was quite capable of taking care of his family. And my grandma didn't let my Mama forget that. Mama was hurt by Grandmama not helping us and her exclusion of her children from the Christmas presents.

"Why!!??" She asked Grandmama.

I heard my Grandmama say, "You should have stayed there with your husband instead of running home to me at the slightest bit of worry. You know I have to take care of all the others."

Bottom line, Mama survived. My mama and Grandmama had an understanding from that day forward. But the rift between them from that day would exist for many years.

I was blessed to witness their relationship transform and blossom into something beautiful during the last years of Mama's life. After they made up, they started calling each other every Sunday. My Mama took care of my Grandmama in her last days. She was her caregiver. But even in her care of my Grandmama, my mama was being cared for too. They were happy to be together in these last days.

I am grateful that the cycle of unresolved conflict and misunderstanding ended with my Mama and her Mother. I hope and pray that me and my daughter and her daughter will always communicate and work through our challenges. I pray for and honor these womanly relations. I will earnestly try to always heal and seal the fundamental and revered connection between me and mine.

I later learned a bit more of my Grandmama's story. This helped me to see why she walked in the toughness I once thought was her being mean. I can't begin to express the magnitude of her story. But I continue to be in awe of my Mama and Grandmama's relationship. Perhaps that will be another book. What I'll say for now is that their relationship had a great impact on my relationship with my mother. While my mother was in the process of understanding and healing their relationship, I am thankful that she tried to be mindful of her relationship with her own daughters.

I also understand now that my Grandmama had to be tough. She was a very beautiful woman. She had skin the color of black coffee with beautiful white teeth, slick black hair and a cocky smile. According to my Daddy, she was the most beautiful woman in the community. I got the impression that Grandmama had to be strong to survive. She was not going to be stepped on nor taken advantage of because of her beauty. She always walked with her head high. She was a nurse by trade. Being the ultimate caregiver, everyone came to her for support and solace. She took care of her children's children, her husband and was a support to her relatives. She took care of the elderly and the veterans in the local rehabilitation facility at St Mary's. Her gift to me was teaching me to be a caregiver with pride and a strong work ethic. She did not complain about her job. She was humble when she spoke about it. She was the first one up in the morning and the last to go to bed. She was dedicated to her work.

That was her calling and she answered that call in everything she did. She was strong, just like the dark black coffee she relished.

Grandmama traveled to Atlanta for my college graduation to celebrate me. I was surprised, honored and a bit surprised. I was still cautious about her until the period in my life when I began having my own children.

I will never forget the time my family and I went home for a family reunion in July, the hottest month of the year in Florida. I was so used to living in the cool altitude of Colorado that I had incredible difficulty breathing in Florida. I was six months pregnant which added to my discomfort. I complained the entire time.

On occasion, I would see Grandmama just watching me. I did not know if she was annoyed with my whining or was just looking after me. After a long hot day we left the reunion party left the hotel and everyone made their way to our matriarch's home. Grandmama did not have an air conditioner. That made my visit there almost unbearable. When I could take no more, I had to call a cousin to pick me up and take me to the coolness of her home.

Just as I was leaving, my Grandmama said, "What's the matter? You too good to stay at my house?" I was emotionally paralyzed and deeply hurt. Me and my pregnant self left in tears. My mama tried to soother me by telling me, "She didn't mean any harm. She's just outspoken."

Thankfully, we flew back to Colorado where I could breathe again. Three am in the morning, two days after being back in Colorado, I was awakened by a phone call from my Grandmama. She said, "Sister, now, I want to tell you that I didn't mean any harm about what I said when you left my house. I was just so thrilled to have you there. Admiring you becoming a woman—I guess my disappointment didn't come out right. I guess I'm still trying to learn how to say things soft and straight." She asked for my forgiveness, told me she loved me and said how proud she was of me. I knew she was sincere. My anger and hurt transitioned to forgiveness.

Grandmama introduced me to what it means to express authentic beauty and love. To be yourself, speak your mind but to try and add a little gentleness. Grandmama had great power and presence yet was often misunderstood because of her tough demeanor.

Grandmama's willingness to admit her error inadvertently taught me about my own majesty. How I need to be myself but to remember being our self is an evolving journey. We have to balance being who we are with gentleness. My lesson was to see me in my majesty and embrace it despite my imperfections.

As I mentioned before, Grandmama also taught me the importance of having a strong work ethic. In her profession as a nurse she took pride in every aspect of her work. From how she dressed to how she performed when she was on duty. Her uniform was the whitest, most starched, cleaned and pressed Nurse's uniform I ever saw. She polished her shoes the night before. The white polish made those shoes look like new even though the therapeutic soles were wearing down on the edges. Grandmama was a humble servant. Through her I learned you can serve and still be powerful. I stand in my power with the work I do. My profession, my vocation is interlaced with my life's purpose of showing up to care and tend to the needs of others. Also, do not assume someone does not need your help because they seem powerful, it could just be an assumption. Bow and be humble to the needs of others, even if they seem strong. Your majesty is in their majesty. Grandmama also taught me that you are not too great or powerful to bow in grace. We should all be humble enough to ask for forgiveness when appropriate.

Her majesty,
My Majesty standing with stamina, power and strength
Powerful to be humble.
*That is the sweetness of Honey….****thelma craig***

73

Chapter 9
Cuz Billie – Vulnerability

When I was a little girl, I wanted to grow up and be a woman that switched. By switch I mean swish your hips side to side with graceful moves when you walk. I'm talking about a slow, steady, smooth sashay. I thought that was the attractive way to present yourself when you show up in the world. I wanted to be a woman that was pure elegance in every way. I wanted to walk and move with all my womanness!

I would often practice switching sometimes after Cuz Billie would visit. I'd stand in the mirror and move my hips side to side just like her. Cuz Billie, was my Mother's cousin. She always showed up beautiful and graceful. I was in awe of her because of how she loved and revered my mama and the way they expected love and support from each other.

Cuz Billie was placed in my life to show me how to appreciate and value the right relationships. But there were other lessons I learned from her. Namely, what I did not want in a relationship with a man. I did not and would not be a woman who tolerated abuse. I would always expect love and demand respect. In this You too movement, we see there are things we need to know early in our girlhood. Don't let nobody mistreat you, physically or mentally. And support each other, where we are in growth.

Although she was fragile, thin and passive, Cuz Billie loved her family, her babies. My Mama had a great connection to this woman. I used to wonder why

Cuz Billie may have stayed an abusive relationship with her husband knowing that my Mama had her back. Both then and now I refuse to judge people who stay in abusive relationships.

In the age of the #metoo and #timesup movement, I often think of her and how powerless she must have felt. After a major episode with her abuser, when her body was covered with black and blue marks, she would call my mother, crying hysterically. My mama would get so mad that she would pack us kids in the car and drive through the Florida National Forest to see about her cousin. My Mama was too mad to cry. She was hurting for Billie. I saw this look many times. But she did not judge or criticize her cousin for her situation. She was determined to support her and love her into loving herself more. She would arrive to her cousin's house, take one look at her, hold her tight and cry with her. Within minutes, Cuz Billie was able to make it through the forest back to our house with her babies in tow. Her and Mama would laugh and cry all the way home. My Mama was the one to console her back to reasonable health.

Not long after Cuz Billie and us kids got settled in, her husband would show up. He'd knock on the door angry, drunk and wild. After a wild exhibition from her husband outside the door, Billie would always open the door to let him in. He'd grab her bruised arm and try to pull her outside, when she was out of reach of my mama.

Mama would hear the commotion, come into the living room , walk over to that short stubby man, put her finger in his face and say, "If you touch my cousin again I will beat the shit out of you."

Mama didn't have a chance to beat him. After several episodes of battering and driving through the forest to see about her cousin, Cuz Billie passed away. She died shortly after the birth of her last baby. I wondered or intuitively I felt that the beatings had damaged her spirit and she just couldn't take it anymore.

I never understood why Cuz Billie kept going back for the turbulence. She kept having babies too. He beat her so bad when she was pregnant, I cringe. I don't know what she died of. That sweet lady died and left her children. Her sweet mother became their mother. As far as I know, they all grew u to be great people.

My hurt over her dying that way taught me to be aware of men who want to hurt you. I also learned to listen to trusted friends that God puts in your life to be there for you during you worst predicaments. My interest in supporting women who are caught in the throes of domestic violence was revealed when I went to Cuzin Billie's funeral. I think hers was the first funeral I had ever attended. Her beautiful curls cascaded over her shoulders as she lay in the pink coffin. I wondered how we could have helped this beautiful soul in her most heartbreaking predicament.

My Great Uncle--my great big Uncle held my hand and walked with me down the clapboard church aisle with the funeral procession. He must've known I was afraid and confused. But mostly I was sad for my

Mama. She must have felt an enormous sense of failure that she couldn't save or protect her Cuz Billie her with her love and devotion.

I was sad for Cuz Billie because she had been unable to grab the life preserver that was given to her. It's hard to understand the myriad of reasons why women stay in abusive relationships. But all we can do is respect their choice and be there for the ones who do have the strength to leave.

Some women stay because they want to be loved and their abuser's love is all they've ever known. Some women believe their abuser will hurt or kill them or their children if they leave. Some believe they cannot afford the change. Most women are simply stuck in the never-ending cycle of abuse and consistent apologies from their perpetrator.

What did this beautiful soul teach me? Support your Sister Friends. I cherish the sister love I saw between my mama and her cousin. I am thankful for the lesson I learned from Billie that violence and abuse is not love and that abuse can kill your spirit. I am deeply thankful to have learned what I do not want for myself in being a woman. I will protect myself and support others in those abusive situations. I will always sashay my womanly hips, moving with grace in honor of the memory of my Cuz Billie.

Gentle soul, sweet and mild
Know that you are endangered
Rebuke things that do not serve and bless you
*You are love.....**thelma craig***

Chapter 10
Marty – Sister in LOVE

My sister-in-law Marty endured tremendous struggle and pain. Yet, she was always there to support and managed to help me relieve the pain of others.

I've heard horror stories about sister in laws. I was fortunate not to have experienced that horror. I shout hallelujah chile' for the blessing of Marty in my life! I admired her from the moment I met her. It was like I'd known her all my life.

When you hear post-partum depression stories, you never think it will happen to you. I still don't know if it did. I just know that I had a living angel by my side after I birthed both of my children. It was a blessing to have someone there to give me womanly life support after having a baby. She had three of her own and raised three wonderful and great sons.

Marty was there for me after every birth. She always came two or three weeks after a baby was born. It was always the right time. I know the fear of being a new Mom and experiencing body changes can be overwhelming. She came with a smile—she came with laughter. She came just at the time I needed while I was at the edge of the abyss. The first order of business was to make sure I got up, had a warm breakfast, a shower and relief from the daily routine of caring for the babies. She would always take me shopping or out for lunch. Sometimes with the babies, sometimes not.

"Girl, you got to fix yourself up. She would say. You got to accessorize with earrings and bracelets. You got to get new makeup and the latest lipstick. You can't let yourself go. That man will leave you if you don't keep yourself fixed up. And you don't want to abandon yourself"

I knew she meant well even though some of her advice was a little outdated and slightly sexist. Marty introduced me to the best bubble baths and bath oils.

"You got to pamper yourself and take care of you," she gently admonished.

She made sure I had enough money to replenish my makeup, get a fresh hairdo and matching shoes. Even if I was dressed to relax around the house, she made sure I looked good.

There were times I found out that Marty was struggling financially when she returned from one her nightingale visits to supporting me and my family. Yet, she sacrificed herself. She expended energy to encourage and affirm me. She created a safe space for me to talk about anything. We talked about marriage, sex, love and life. She was very open about all things private. She shared the good and bad of being with a man and being a mother. She always shared with me the importance of not letting yourself go. She taught me how to treat yourself to the little niceties that being a woman should come with. And one is not to allow yourself to be abused in any way.

Things like buying scented candles and sachets of potpourri to keep sweet aromas around you. She loved bric-a-brac and collected bracs of cuteness, butterflies and especially sailboats. She loved sailboats. I wonder today if this was her way to escape. She would stare and admire the sailboats made with all types of materials. I found it amazing how looking at a small piece of art made her want to sail into a peaceful place and brought a bright smile to her face.

Marty taught me that these little selfish indulgences were a fine way to take care of yourself. Today, I too collect art. I collect items that bring a smile to my heart. Things like bird houses, horses and masks.

Marty was like a shiny penny you find unexpectedly, and it brings good luck. She brought good love. She was new money to my soul. I will never forget her *lucky visit* as I used to call it.

I remember her asking upon arrival if our town had a dog track. I told her yes, but I had never gone. I explained that I didn't have the money to spare nor did I know how to play. She'd brush me off and said, "You don't need to know. Let's go!"

And so we went. And I have to admit, I was a bit excited when we arrived at the track. I remember looking around in anticipation. People had desperate looks on their face like they were worried if their dog would come in first, second or third. She commenced with a lesson on how to play the dog races. She asked me what three numbers I had in mind. I thought, what a coincidence. In a recent and quite vivid dream I had dreamed free and clear, the numbers 7-5-6.

She commenced to share with me the "rules of the game". She explained me what straight and box bets meant. She asked me if I was confident in the number to play it both straight and in the box. Among other tips, she explained what Trifecta meant. I placed my numbers confidently. I won the Trifecta for fifteen hundred dollars! She won just as much using the numbers I dreamed. This was during the time we were living from paycheck to paycheck, caring for two little ones, often not knowing if we would have to contact the utility company to make arrangements to pay.

We were starving for some fun and some light in our finances. When we arrived home with our winnings, I rang the doorbell. My husband answered a little grumpy because he was sleeping, and he was certain I had my house key.

I began to pull one hundred dollar bills out of my bosom slowly, making my husband grab me in excitement. My lucky guardian knew that we were in need of a break and I was blessed with exactly what we needed.

Marty's encouragement and essential lessons in self-care were invaluable. Her presence blessed my husband and I with the money to take a badly needed family vacation to New Mexico. Self-care was our intention. We always had fun with Marty.

Marty has been diagnosed with Alzheimer. We visited her recently. She remembers us and know us. We were able to say: I love you: and she returned the sentiment. It saddens me that she is not a full vibrant self. She is at the top of my prayer list. My prayer for her in this state of her life is to have peace of mind and peace in her spirit. She deserves to be cared for because she cared enough to ensure that others cared for themselves. I am sure God will answer that prayer above and beyond.

You lifted me
You added the polish to shine
Bright light in my face and my heart
*Your accents were jewelry for my soul…**thelma craig***

Chapter 11
Letha Ann – Navigator

Have you ever met somebody who just met somebody who reached out to that person because they knew they needed a job? Have you ever been in a position where you could refer and support someone on their path and offer blessings for their Journey? That was how I came to know Letha Ann. Someone I knew had a friend who was looking for a position. They needed a lift. I was proud of the role I was serving in at the time. It was a position that allowed me to refer someone for a blessing. I had it like that. Letha Ann not only got the position, but I knew immediately after she was hired, that I had made a friend...

Many years later, Letha Ann gave me a gift for my fiftieth birthday. It was a painting on a medium-sized canvas with striking earth tones of orange, red and gold. The painting had a quote that read, "I am not afraid of storms for I have learned how to sail my ship." My mind raced when I read the quote. I thought--*no, I have not learned. I still need your nurturing, support and guidance.*"

When I first read the quote, I was devastated. It was that fear of abandonment feeling I get when I assume someone is trying to leave me. I had not yet learned to trust God totally.

I continued unwrapping my present and read the quote on the painting again. Did this mean she was letting me go? Would she no longer be the ears for my crises or the one to sooth my frightened soul?

I looked up to Letha Ann. From the moment I met her, I knew she had something to teach me and that she was a Godsend. I felt safe with her. She not only taught me scriptures, she shared soulful, engaging stories with me. Her stories were beautifully layered in scripture and they corresponded with the worries I had experienced. I was always in awe of that.

I remember coming to Letha Ann with a fear I had. I was in conflict with a person. I knew this person wasn't one hundred percent for me but I was afraid to sever ties. I shared with Letha Ann that sometimes I was afraid to lose people because I thought one day, I might need them. I assumed that day would come at a time when my life was hard to bear alone. I was also afraid of losing my parents in death. That was a fear that had been with me for a long time.

I held fast to the idea that I needed to hold onto relationships that did not serve me because I thought those people would be there in my time of need. Letha Ann had a scripture for me. She said, "Isaiah 41:10. Fear not, for I am with thee. Be not dismayed, for I am thy God. I will strengthen thee. Yea, I will help thee. Yea, I will uphold thee with the right hand of my righteousness."

After reading that scripture, I understood that the word of God was true. If we got in touch with and built a relationship with God, if we know our own soul, the Holy Spirit would speak to us during challenging moments. I had gotten that scriptural lesson from my mom and others earlier in life but it really clicked when I talked about it with Letha Ann.

As we got closer, whenever I had a problem happening in my life, I ran to Letha Ann. She would share a scripture and then tell me a rich story that ended with a reflection. Things like, *God will give you everyone and everything you need in your moment of fear.*

She told me the story of how she lost her mother and sister a few weeks from each other. She told me about the pain she felt but quoted a scripture that comforted her during that turbulent period of her life.

"God said, The Holy Spirit dwells in her." That simple scripture had gotten her through.

She also told me that she did not feel alone when she was in the thick of grieving such tremendous losses. When I asked her why she said, "God said, do not fear because I am with thee."

We continued our discussions during what we had started calling our *wine time.* Sometimes *wine time* talks happened in her office behind closed doors. It worked out perfect because we worked in the same department. I felt it was really meant to be that we worked in the same area during that time in my life.

After I had a difficult encounter with a co-worker or supervisor, I would find my way to Letha Ann for one of our *wine time* talks.

After twenty plus years of the gift of Letha Ann's friendship, I thought the painting was her way of saying she was letting me go. Maybe she had nothing else to teach me about sailing the ship called my life.

Letha Ann was and is a pillar of wisdom. She was a woman whose shoulder I laid my head on numerous times during moments of distress. We also shared fun times. The joys of family life. Our lives were very similar—I had noted that from the beginning. Letha Ann had a wonderful and devoted husband just like I did. She and her husband also had a daughter and a son the same distance in age as my daughter and son. Letha Ann's husband was a US Marine just like mine. Letha Ann was also a Christian woman who walked with a sense of love, forgiveness and in the *lean not to your own understanding* Christian consciousness.

After months of fuming and being mad at Letha Ann about the message I *thought* she gave me with her gift, I humbled my prideful self and admitted I was upset. To my amazement, she laughed and explained her leaving was not the intention of the gift. The message was meant to encourage me to recognize my own strength and that she believed I was going in a good direction on my Journey and in my relationship with God. I will always be grateful for my conversations with Letha Ann… I understand now that God places Godly women in your life to share his word and reinforce his promises.

The waters are healing
The mountains are a power source
You have great strength
*In You I see the Power and the Glory…****thelma craig****

Chapter 12
Millie – Admirer

I went to visit my 96-year-young friend today. She is still as feisty as ever.

As I sat there talking with her, she said, "I didn't plan for this. What am I going to do at this age? No Thelma, I don't want to live to be 100 years old." She laughed and gave me that eye. The eye that told me she loved me, liked me and wanted me to understand what she was saying. It is truly a blessing when you admire and like yourself; and that person admire and like you too.

Millie was a proud southern woman who at an early age, had moved to Colorado with her husband. She was far from home but went on to master living in another state. I loved her southern charm. She always blessed my heart when I was in her presence. She was a librarian and was such a proper, gentile woman. There is so much in her story that needs to be shared.

Millie was a pillar of power and strength. I remember visiting her with another wise woman. I had mentioned to the woman what Millie told me about feeling like she was ready to go because she couldn't think of anything else, she could do at 100 years old. The woman told me, "There is always something we can do at every age. She has us coming over to sit with her, giving her our undivided attention. That's doing something for us and is a blessing in and of itself. We're having a marvelous time listening to her— laughing at our comments. She is giving us delight, lifting us up and showing us how to be graceful as we age."

My 96-year-old friend sat there talking and enjoying the lunch we brought her. She had requested *JOE's Barbeque.* We ate, laughed, talked and listened. She hung on to our every word—partly because her hearing was diminishing but mostly because she delighted in listening to us talk. We were animated and always excited to talk to her. We even got up to describe what we were talking about. We gestured and acted out the scenario. She laughed until tears were running down her face.

During our future visits, she started carrying a little box of tissues to wipe the fluid leaking from her eyes, nose and mouth. I knew that meant she wasn't well. She still laughed and we continued to indulge her. I think we exaggerated and embellished the stories so she that could laugh even harder. Hearing her laughter was pure heaven.

We knew she loved us and that she liked us too. She admired me with a fierceness. She admired us all. I thought about her when I was planning my 40th birthday celebration which was a High Tea. It was a time in my life when I was discovering so much about myself. I invited Millie and twenty-four other fabulous women to attend the party.

Millie brought her best sister friend, another great woman in my life. They shared how they had been friends for over sixty years. Her friend was ten years younger than her. Each of the women at the party shared a piece of their stories. Special moments about their mentors, mothers, grandmothers or friends. There wasn't a dry eye in the house. Everyone expressed how much they treasured the tea party. When I walked Millie to the door and helped her put on her coat, she thanked me. She looked up at me from her short stature, stared lovingly into my eyes and said, "I sure hope you like yourself, because I sure do."

The last time I visited Millie, she was getting restless. She said that she had been dreaming about her sister for several weeks. After being solemn for few seconds, I asked what the dream was about? I asked about the scene she saw. I also asked her what she thought the dream meant. Millie said, "She just appeared to me. I think I heard her calling me. Maybe she was saying it's time to join her."

I recalled when my Great Grandma sat on the porch in her rocker and responded to the greeting from others asking about her well-being. As far back as I could remember she always responded, "Just sitting here waiting for the chariot to come take me home."

Millie's reflection reminded me of my Great Grandma. Millie passed away 3 weeks after that last visit.

Sweet laughter full of tears
Smiles your face is smeared
How blessed I am to have experienced
The joy of all your years….thelma craig

Chapter 13
Miss Pearl – Entrepreneur

Miss Pearl ran the best and only soul food restaurant in Ocala, Florida, my small-town birthplace. Miss Pearl was known across the country, from the south to the east coast. People traveled miles to visit her café. It was a hole in the wall at the top of a barbershop and local bar on Main Street and Broadway. This was my Daddy's hangout strip after work. I knew it because on paydays, my Mama would load us kids in the car and drive downtown to the Broadway strip. She would park in the car lot and ask one of us kids to go check the barbershop or the bar for Daddy. We did as we were told while she waited with bated breath. We always found him in the chair or on the barstool. When he saw us, he would embrace us and tell everyone in the building who we were. His babies. He was always in celebratory mood when he saw us enter *his* establishments.

He would tell us, *"Go get yo' mama out of the car."* We would climb the rickety stairs to *Miss Pearl's Soul Food Restaurant.* Miss Pearl was more than just a businesswoman to our father. She was his friend. So much so that he named her my brother's Godmother. I think she knew my Daddy before he knew himself. They had a profound connection. He spent a lot of time around her. You could feel the love they had for each other. She was like an auntie to him. She wasn't old enough to be his mother or grandmother but just right to be his aunt, a close second to a mother.

He loved to support her business. The shop was Main Street for Blacks in that era. It was a block lined with Black-owned bars, barbershops, shoeshine stands and pawnshops.

You had to enter Miss Pearl's through the back ally and up the fire escape stairs. It was a warm, cozy and most importantly, safe hideout. Miss Pearl knew about the numbers. Gambling was cultural entertainment during that time. I appreciate now how we found ways to supplement our income back then. I would see folks passing little bits of paper and tightly folded money to the bookie.

Miss Pearl's restaurant was the place to go on payday. She did not have a written menu. After she kissed and hugged us all she would smile, get a piece of paper and pen, and run down the menu items in song. I mean it was like rap song or spoken word. It had a melody and a cadence.

"Today I got cabbage, collards, turnips, Black-eye peas, candy yams, fried chicken, smothered chicken, fried and smothered pork chops. You know I got corn bread and crackling too. I just can't have black-eyed peas without candied yams."

That was sweet music to my little ears and stomach. It stuck with me. After she sang that tune, it was as if she did a ditty and cakewalked to the kitchen to prepare your plate. Oh my God--the food was delicious. This was our treat on Daddy's payday. She knew how to serve and she knew how to cook. Her food was delicious. People came from miles around. She was an expert in her craft.

Of course, he spent a lot of time there. He was devoted and always supported Miss Pearl. After all, she was my brother's Godmother. She just smiled when my Mom or Daddy mentioned his name. Then she'd ask, "How's my boy?" I don't think she heard a word, because her smile just took over the space and the conversation. She was imagining his look. She was seeing him in her mind and in her heart and soul. Needless to say, she loved herself some brother. She called that.

God only knows how she felt when my father came to tell her that her beloved Godson had died in a car accident. She was still living but weak and homebound by then. I know she loved and cared for children. I had always felt special around her. I didn't think she ever had any kids of her own.

Looking back, I can see now that she was an advocate for children and the struggling. Miss Pearl was a businesswoman. Her restaurant was always filled with the community. She had passion for the people she served food to. She had passion for the work of food service. Any motherless child hanging out around her establishment would certainly get fed. Miss Pearl imparted in me that preparing food for folks was an act of love. While she was in business to earn a living, she had great love and devotion to serving people. She was a queenly entrepreneur.

Miss Pearl created a business centered around her love of feeding people. A business where she could also be an advocate for her people. I admired that. She was a true pearl... She is a woman to be hailed, admired and supported. Let's support each other when we are being our creative and business selves. Being and entrepreneur required support from us

If we are to succeed in our life's purpose, whether in business, art or vocation, we must work in it as a labor of love.

Singing, I got greens
I got peas
I got hope
I got love
I got cornbread
*For your soul, baby......***thelma craig**

Chapter 14
Debbie –The Neighbor

I heard my Daddy say one time, I love my Black women. A white woman doesn't hold a candle to Black women. He called us sapphires. My Daddy was old school cool. To this day I think of that comment from him and wonder if it was a teaching moment. Was he trying to make me feel good about my Black skin? Was he trying to assure me that he loved Black women? That I didn't have to worry about my black skin or concern myself with where I stand as a woman in this racist world. That I don't ever have to compare myself to White women....

At the time, with all the negative images in magazines, TV commercials and other places that many Black girls had to sublimely endure, my father's reassurance was critical. Knowing that my father cherished Black women meant the world to me. My Daddy was a subtle teacher like that. He called me Black Gal. No one in the world could call me that except him. He defended it and he made sure I defended it too. But I tell you the truth, the White lady that lived across the street captured his heart.

He loved himself some Debbie. And now I love her. I always feel that he presented her to me to look out for me after his death. And she was a White, Republican, New Englander, a dog lover and what some would call a red neck. She had the cutest dog. All my life I knew my Daddy did not like dogs but when I visited him during his last couple of years, Debbie would have her cute little Beagle in tow.

My Daddy grinned ear-to-ear when that dog wagged his tail to greet him. My mouth flew wide open when I saw my Daddy pet the dog and allow him into his house. The dog's tail was wagging. He was happy to see my Daddy. It was like the dog was smiling and I saw my Daddy was smiling too.

Debbie would always knock on my Daddy's door to see how he was doing. She would bring a plastic bowl of something that she made to share with him. She would bake blueberry muffins and take them to him while they were still warm. I would get a call from my Daddy shortly after the delivery. I could hear his smile.

"Hey, your friend just bought over some hot muffins for me."

He was smacking in my ear—one of my pet peeves. Somehow it didn't bother me because he sounded so happy. I can tell you that if he ever was smitten or interested in being with a White woman in his early days—It would've been Debbie. She came into my life on an occasion several years before my Daddy died. I was visiting my Daddy after his wife died. Debbie was the neighbor across the street from which you could see the entire parameter of my Daddy's house. And she watched out for him like a hawk. She had a heart for my Daddy. And I liked her right way.

I can apply that sentiment to my Daddy's favorite saying, "You like em, I like em." He liked her husband too. Her husband testified at my Daddy's funeral

.

Debbie and her husband were the only White folks present at his funeral. I am certain they didn't mind the exclusion. They were proud to be there to say goodbye. They cried their hearts out. Debbie's husband got up to speak before the mourners. He told the story of how he first met my Daddy living across the street from him. He shared how every day, for several weeks after my Daddy moved across from his house, they watched each other from their garages. He would look at my Daddy and my Daddy would look at him. They didn't speak, wave or nod to each other. They just eyed each other. They peered from the windows. Finally, one day, they both got up and walked toward each other.

Daddy said they met in the middle of the road. The middle of the road was powerfully stated by her husband in describing the beginning of a great neighborly friendship. He said they looked each other square in the eye and shook hands. From that day on they cared for Daddy. They watched out for him and he watched out for them. That's when that beautiful neighborly truth came to being. Debbie became a mainstay in my Daddy's life. Daddy found it easy to trust her, even though we were from different backgrounds. She would tease and admonish him if he wasn't taking care of himself. Because I was thousands of miles away, I appreciated their friendship. She reassured me that she was looking out. She made sure I had all her phone numbers in case I was concerned about my Daddy as his health was diminishing. She made sure he knew she was looking out for him.

During his failing health, she became ill and had to go to the hospital. When I gave him the news, I saw his eyes water. But then I thought, Daddy *don't cry*. I had only seen him cry a few times.

Then he said, "I wish I was in the hospital instead of her. I don't like to think of her suffering."

She survived and he perked up.

She was among my strongest supporters when my Daddy passed. She was one of the people God placed in my life to see me through the grief. What did I learn from this bouncy, spicy White woman? How to be a neighbor and how to love thy neighbor.

I have always had special relationships with the White women God has placed on my path. They know who they are and what they mean to me. Debbie was the one who reminded me of the value that I place in all my friends, Black, White and Latina and women of different cultural backgrounds.

Debbie made me think how the generational experience of racism impacts our relationships. We are often blinded by our misunderstanding of people of different ethnic and cultural backgrounds. We grow up learning to distrust people of other races. Debbie helped open my mind to exploring friendships with people from every walk of life.

Debbie, being who she is as a loving soul, was there at the right time to *Love Thy Neighbor*. Debbie, through her love and support of my father, taught me that we should cherish and recognize people for who they are and not judge them on the color of their skin. Trust that heartfelt relationships do not have a color...

I see you over there
Differences abound
You see me here
I know we are connected
*I know you care…..***thelma craig**

Chapter 15
Mrs. Annie Lee – A Faith

Miss Annie Lee was the one that told me, "Always get a man that loves you more than you love him."

I responded with wonderment, "How do you know something like that?"

She went on to say, "As a woman, I just know. Oh, and that doesn't mean you don't love him. No baby, it's that you can feel the magnitude of his love for you. And it's greater than yours."

I said, "Okay. I'll try and really pay attention."

Miss Annie Lee was my co-worker at the nursing home. We always made time to talk during the breaks. It was the best part of the job. She was the lead resident staff nurse. She was a true caregiver because she cared about the residents and the staff. She cared for all the people around her. She said she wanted to make sure people in her life and path were cared for and that she could be a light. She was a beacon of light for me during a vulnerable time in my life.

Working at the nursing home was my first employment after graduating from college. It was a job and it helped me pay my rent. She was not my immediate supervisor but if felt like she was. She trained and guided me at the beginning of my work career.

My supervisor was a tyrant. She was a mean, nasty woman who wore bright red lipstick and a full-on nurse uniform with the pill hat. Her dingy, matted gray hair would stick out from beneath the hat. Her red lipstick was always smeared on her teeth and face. I knew my supervisor was out to destroy me.

But Miss Annie Lee was always there like a life preserver. She assured me that my supervisor would not destroy me.

"She's treating folks like that because she's miserable and feels destroyed within herself." Miss Annie said convincingly. I wasn't convinced by Miss Annie's words, but I did calm down a little.

The year I was planning my wedding, Miss Annie Lee gave me a bridal shower at work in the employee lounge. She showered me with her wisdom of being a married woman. We talked about everything from marriage to work and of course, God. She was an admirable woman. She stood tall, regal and confident. She was confident when she cared for the residents and when she interacted with the staff. I often asked her why she wasn't supervisor. That's when she told me about discrimination and unfairness in the workplace.

Miss Annie Lee was not discouraged. She had a great work ethic and expected to see everybody doing their work properly. She was mesmerizing. She wore her beautiful black hair in a French Roll. Her uniform was perfectly starched, neat and white as her pearly teeth. Her cocoa dark skin glowed and was smooth as a baby's bottom. She was beautiful. And I saw myself in her beauty. She made me appreciate my dark skin, another confirmation. I just knew she was placed in my life for a reason. She made coming to work during the midnight shift feel like it was part of my destiny. I loved working at that Nursing home because I enjoyed her company.

Miss Annie Lee taught me how to appreciate my work. What a blessing for my first employment immediately after college. I looked forward to finishing our rounds, after all the residents were tucked in—so I could sit and relax and talk or listen to Miss Annie. We had to make sure that the supervisor was on another floor or asleep. It was such relief when the mean red lipstick lady no longer worked on the same floor. She was mean to the core and that frightened me to my core. But Miss Annie Lee kept telling me not to let her get to me. S o I tried not to.

Miss Annie Lee was a profound speaker. She spoke gently, with intention and with a strong tone. I think she knew she had an impact on my young, eager heart and mind. She always called me her baby girl.

Miss Annie Lee brought great home-cooked snacks to the table. We would sit and talk all night unless the monitor alerted us to a resident in crisis or the mean lady supervisor was on the floor. I was so afraid of my supervisor that I used to have stomach cramps when I arrived for the shift. I thought I was developing an ulcer. My stomach felt raw. I shivered every time I was in her presence.

One night on the late shift, Miss Annie Lee made me some tea, ordered me to relax and we talked the nightshift away. She said, "Baby girl, you can't let people get inside you like that." She took a jar off the nurse's counter, the one that held the wooden throat thongs. Then she took the reflex tool and said, "You see this jar? If I hit it in the inside with this instrument, it will easily shatter and break. If I hit it on the outside like so, it's harder to shatter and break. So, don't let nobody hit you from your insides. Stop letting that woman get to the inside of you. Try to understand, it is not always about you. Forgive her and be gentle with yourself."

From that day on, I told myself I was not going to let the supervisor break me. I tried to understand what she might be going through. I tried to feel compassion for her misery and let go. The next night, I came to work, ready to be strong. I was ready to face the supervisor with my stomach tight and my mind on protecting me. I was going to greet her with a new attitude. I arrived for my night shift and greeted the resident assistant on the shift before me. She gave me the report and left.

I forgot to ask where the Supervisor was. She was usually at the counter when I arrived. I moved through the hall peeping in on the residents in my charge that night. I went back to the nurse's station and still did not see the supervisor. I felt relieved but was a little disappointed. I was ready to try out my new attitude on her. I was going to be strong, positive and take care of myself. Like Miss Annie Lee and I had discussed, I was not going to let her break me on the inside. I planned to greet her with resolve.

For some reason the residence floor was peaceful and quiet. When I went to the nurse's lounge the lights were off and the coffee was brewing. I noticed Miss Annie Lee sitting in the corner relaxing and drinking her coffee. I saw those pearly white teeth when she smiled.

I turned on the lights and asked, "What's going on? Why are the lights out? It seems so peaceful around here? Oh, and where is the supervisor?" Miss Annie Lee got up, refreshed her coffee and said,

"Sit down, baby."
I was ready for her to tell me something like, I was losing my job. I thought perhaps the supervisor gave Miss Annie Lee the task of telling me I was fired. I figured she was too mean and inconsiderate to tell me herself.

Before Miss Annie Lee could tell me what she wanted to talk to me about I said, "I'm ready for what you got. I let go. I'm not going to let the supervisor keep me worried or scared." Miss Annie Lee led me to the chair and told me to relax. "Baby, you don't have to be worried anymore.

"The supervisor, Miss Rachet, died today."
I felt a sense of relief but also felt sympathy for her. I was surprised that there was sadness in me about her passing.

Miss Annie Lee became the supervisor. All the staff loved and respected her. She had an impact on us all. I worked there for a few more months. While I was preparing for my wedding, Miss Annie Lee spent many nightshifts talking to me about life, work and marriage. The nursing home became a nursing place for me. I was nurtured and blessed by the supervision of Miss Annie Lee.

I also learned how to let go and know that God has a plan for my life. The mean supervisor lady taught me to know that when people treat you bad, its not always about you. I learned the true meaning of the saying, *misery loves company*. Often times, when people attack you or are so intent on breaking you, it's because they are broken themselves. There is often something going on or wrong in their lives and so they lash out at others to cover up their feelings of pain, hurt or inadequacy. Sometimes they don't even know that they are ill and miserable. And we often take it upon ourselves to be hurt and offended. I understand now that people will often impose their hurts on you unknowingly. I learned to strengthen my discernment and keep watch over my heart when I feel that people are trying to hurt me.

Mrs. Annie Lee was a manager and leader who took pride in her position. She nurtured the patients and everyone in her care. She was a work friend for my soul. God puts us in places where we get what we need to thrive. What better place than the workplace? We spend a lot of time there. I will never forget the blessings of working with her and the way she cared for everyone she interacted with.

I hold out my hand
I open my heart
Make me, don't break me
*Touch me, wake me....**thelma craig***

Chapter 16
Miss Gruggs – First Impression

Miss Gruggs, my first-grade teacher, truly deserves to be listed among the women who helped me to become the woman I am today. She ranks high in my life because of her loving, kind and edifying way of teaching kids. I believe she showed up at that little, colored, segregated school to teach us in a loving way. Black teachers back then wore their purpose on their shoulders. This was the sixties. They knew we had some disadvantages in primary education. Our tools, books and materials were limited but we had a tremendous amount of love and devotion from our teachers. My sweet little school was painted sea green with black trim. It had a steeple with a bell on the top layer of the roof. Miss Gruggs was beautiful. She had dark cocoa skin and was simply an elegant, sweet smelling woman. All the kids liked her. She was pleasant and seemed to smile all day long. She was excited when the kids participated in class dialogue. She listened to us and made everything seem like it was the best thing she ever heard. Looking back, I know it was a huge blessing to have a dark skinned, smart, loving, beautiful Black woman as my first-grade teacher. Miss Gruggs always dressed nice. She wore beautiful dresses and high heels shoes. She didn't mind hugging and touching the children even if it meant her risking getting dirty. Especially after recess when we were all sweaty and muddy from that Florida humidity. When the kids teased me, all I had to do was look at Miss Gruggs and immediately I felt better. She reminded me of me. And that meant I was beautiful too. Miss Gruggs taught me the importance of having Black teachers teach Black kids in their early years at an educational institution. I will never forget the time I came running into the school before the bell rang. I ran into her arms and told her about the horrifying experience I had walking to school with my schoolmates. We had run through the graveyard. The kids were teasing this man that walked on crutches and had one leg. It's not uncommon for kids to tease each other and kids often make fun of people who are different in ways that really stick out. When we called him the Shaky Leg Man, he would shake and wiggle his stub leg toward us and make us run for our lives. I remember how his right pants leg was folded and pinned back. His crutches had tape on them like they had been repaired. Every time we saw the Shaky Leg Man we'd would run screaming through the Bethune Cookman Heights Cemetery into the school. I'm not sure why the Shaky Leg Man scared me so much but today I know I had and have nothing to fear because I walk in the shadow of death and fear no evil. I remember feeling like death was chasing me as I ran into the school. I saw Miss Gruggs smiling and standing at the massive door, waving and greeting other kids arriving at school. I ran into her arms with my tear stained, dusty face. I had a few bruises from falling a couple of times as I ran to the school. Miss Gruggs face quickly changed to concern. She hugged me then lead me to her classroom. The other teachers watched us pass and continued to greet the kids arriving for the school day. Miss Gruggs helped clean off the dirt and dust from the unpaved road through the graveyard. She dabbed my bruises with a paper towel as I sat at her desk shaken and teary eyed.

"Calm down and tell me what happened." She said as I slowed my breathing.

I still couldn't talk. The nervousness had me speechless. I told her I had to pee. She led me to the girl's bathroom. Afterwards, as we walked back to the classroom, I told her every detail of the experience. She listened intently. "We were skipping through the graveyard. All of a sudden, Mr. Shaky Leg Man appeared in front of us. The kids began to run for our lives after calling him out of his name. I was running as fast as I could. I turned around to see where he was and fell face first onto the dirt road. When I looked up, I could see the unkempt graves and the moss-covered tree branches hanging, almost touching the ground. It scared me. Then I turned around and the Shaky Leg Man was standing over me shaking his stubbed leg. I couldn't cry out. I turned my head toward him, looked him in the eye and saw nothing. He said, "Go on. Giddy up little girl. You gon' be late for school. Get up now and run fast to school. Catch up wit' yo' buddies."

I almost fell again as I got up to run away. I glanced back and he was still standing there smiling at me with a toothless smile. I told Miss Gruggs that I thought I heard him say that he was going to "flunk" me. I meant F me as in have sex with me. But I said the word flunk instead. "I thought, if the Shaky Leg Man catches me, he will flunk me." To that. she smiled then laughed and laughed. She led me down the hall where two other first-grade teachers were waiting outside their classroom door. She told me to tell the other teachers what I told her. After I repeated the, "He was going to flunk me," part of my story, they smiled and cracked up too. I heard them repeat the word flunk several times. They increased their laughter each time they said it. To my dismay, I began to laugh along with them. I didn't know what was so funny but laughing made me feel a little better and calmed my fears. Miss Gruggs led me back to her room and reassured me that I was safe and that they know about the man on the way to school. His name was Mr. Hill. He was a disabled veteran. Miss Gruggs explained to me the challenges that disabled veterans faced and that he didn't intend to do any harm to us. She assured me that he was walking through the neighborhood looking out for the little ones. "Mr. Hill is a World War II veteran. He was injured during the war and they had to take his leg. He's related to a well-known family in the area. He walks the neighborhood looking after the kids as they trek to school. He has no intentions to harm you or your friends." Her explanation made me feel better. She continued. "Mr. Hill is unable to work due to an injury that happened during his service. That's why we call him a disabled veteran". I knew what disabled veteran meant because my Daddy was a Purple Heart, Korean War Veteran. My little heart understood. I felt sorry about teasing Mr. Gruggs. Sometimes when I think about that experience, I think about the scripture *Psalms 23: 4* "*Ye, though I walk through the valley and the shadow of death, I will fear no evil. For thou art with me.*" I realized running through the cemetery, running into Mr. Hill with his one leg, made me think about something gloomy and made me feel like I'd been enveloped by the shadow of death.

Miss Gruggs continued to tell the story of Mr. Hill's life's challenges. I asked questions and after I finished talking, she put her arms around me, stood back and laughed warmly. "And no baby, he was not going to flunk you. She touched my nose and motioned me towards my desk. The kids entered the class. After the bell rang and the kids were seated, Miss Gruggs explained to the kids about Mr. Hill. I learned another lesson through this experience. Sometimes God places people in your path to teach you compassion. Because of my fear of Shaky Leg Man, I learned to have compassion for the real person, Mr. Hill. I initially feared him. He was a stranger. My mom always told us about strangers. But through the experience, I learned how many war veterans were hurt and wounded when they were fighting for our country. Fortunately, Shaky Leg Man had a good heart and soul—such that he looked out for the kids in the neighborhood. He deserved to be honored and respected because he'd fought in the war and returned home injured. Miss Gruggs was a great teacher and inspiration in my life. And me and my fellow students would continue to see Mr. Hill even after we graduated. And some kids continued to call him the Shaky Leg Man.

Touch my mind with your care,

Touch my face with your light bright lessons

Uplift my soul with mesmerizing strength

*Ready me up for victory….**thelma craig***

Chapter 17

Abigail - Seeker

I never felt inferior or less than around my first Jewish friend. I am blessed to have encountered her and other Jewish people in my path that cared about me as much as she did. I can actually name a few. They just always seem to have such flare and compassion. Throughout history I recall hearing myths or rumors about the relationships between African American/ Black people and American Jewish folk.   It really never mattered to me. Whenever I encounter or work with a Jewish person or a project, the chemistry is always there. History does reveal controversy and conflict between Jewish people and people of color. It never bothered or deterred me from befriending or working with a Jewish person. I even Googled the history of these two mighty people and found interesting data in Wikipedia. An article called, "The Civil Rights Act of 1964: A Long Struggle for Freedom." I will save the discussion about this article for another book. Back to Abigail…….

I know that women were placed in my life for a brief time to shine their light on me. I also share my light with other women to be a beacon of light, healing and hope. As a Black girl from the deep south, with all its rich and sordid history, I understand the importance of the support of women from all backgrounds and races. It's a blessing when people from different ethnic backgrounds grow up together. It never occurred to me that I would be BFF's with a White girl or girl from any other race. Even though I am clear about the perils of racism, my innocent mind did not allow such prejudices to stop me from befriending people of other races. I look for the light inside of them. I ask God to help me discern who is for me and who is sent by God to enlighten me. I try to bring and share my light as well. Sometimes people come to be a mirror. To be a reflection and help us identify the best of the qualities in ourselves. It can be hard for women of different backgrounds to trust each other enough to share space. Back when I was growing up, it was not common for people of different races to have deep friendships. But God is in control of whom He places in your life. Not this racist world. And I am grateful for all the different people I have been blessed to experience. I don't like it when people say they don't see color or difference. We are all different and we each bring uniqueness to the relationships. Abigail was not the type to "act" Black. She respected and loved her own culture too much for that. She also respected Black culture. She has a passion for the causes that Black People stand up for and the causes that are important to her own people. She embodied the charge of the "Black Lives Matter," movement. She was intent on helping to facilitate social justice advocacy. I met her while working for the Colorado Health Department. She was always in attendance of workshops, forums and conferences that had a focus on advocacy and education as it relates to health disparity.

Abigail is a seeker. Her being a seeker was what gave me the opening to get to know her. Abigail truly wanted to understand—not because of her race or religion—but because she cared. And I know this because that's how she always made me feel—cared for. Abigail never ceased to amaze me in her efforts to support our community's health issues. She was a facilitator and a convener at some of the events we attended. She was also a beauty. She had full thick course hair that always seem to be in disarray. It was as if she was there to roll up her sleeves and find ways to connect to the community and give support. Every time I saw her, she greeted me with a hug and openly admired my Blackness. She said it with passion. She always complemented me on my beauty and dark skin. She always gave my self-esteem a boost. Abigail is smart, friendly and eager to serve.

Abigail was also proud of her religion. She seemed to be a rebel, but I always felt her deep devotion to her Jewish faith. Abigail also joined a Women's spiritual bible study group that I hosted. All the other women were Black and from Christian backgrounds. For some reason, I was inspired to invite her to this Sister circle. She was more than excited to be a part. She contributed much to the conversation, yet still holding true to herself and her beliefs. She listened, shared and contributed in a way that uplifted us all.

Through Abigail's example, I learned that when you are true to yourself and your faith, your light will shine. Your purpose will show up in places where you are meant to serve. Abigail lit up the room with her light for service. This lesson will always be in my heart.

The wind is strong at will
The breeze revels in the space we are in
I can see the reflection in smiles
I can feel the wind of grace and authenticity
*…..**thelma craig***

Chapter 18
Dr. Melanie – My Advocate

I didn't realize I was ashamed of my mother being a maid until I went away to college and started comparing myself to others and their family backgrounds. Naturally, I was ashamed to share that part of my family history. But my mother not only worked hard, she had an exceptional work ethic. Regardless of her job title, her legacy of service was something to be proud of.

When I went off to college, I was exposed to young people who had more advantages than I. They had parents that went to college and had professions like doctors, lawyers and politicians. I felt so ashamed of myself for feeling ashamed. When I began to love myself, I learned to appreciate my mother for the sacrifices she made. My mother's job allowed her to be able to take care of herself and her kids.   She made her position as a maid seem important and it was. She became a priceless asset to the people she worked for. She was the reason their households functioned properly.

Dr. Melanie was not only my mother's employer, she became a friend to my mother. She helped her expand the purpose of her ministry. They became spiritual sisters. When my mother was at work, they discussed the bible and how the Lord was working in their lives. Eventually, they became each other's spiritual directors. Mama was proud of the relationship and the support she and her employer gave each other. Dr. Melanie was a true missionary and activist rolled in to one tough lady. She was a veterinarian specializing in horses. A loving wife and devoted mother, she loved animals and other helpless creatures.

Dr. Melanie was my first experience with a humanitarian and animal rights activist.

She used to say, "Sister," that's what she called me, "All people are equal."

She was always trying to show and tell me that all White people are not bigoted and racist. On many occasions, she showed me that she cared. Even though she was a privileged, wealthy White woman, it amazed me how she intentionally demonstrated fairness and concern for others.

My mother had worked as a maid off and on for different White families throughout the years of my childhood. But she was more than a maid for Dr. Melanie's' household. She became part of the family. With induction into the family came natural accolades. Don't get me wrong, there were days my mama came home complaining about the demands her boss put on her. Mama would come home and head straight to bed after she checked to see if we completed our chores, cooked our meals and we looked like we were ok. I don't recall her sharing about a racial issue. They had a really powerful and dynamic relationship. My only regret is that I didn't write a book about them before the book, *The Help* was published. There are so many stories from *The Help* that reminded me of mama and Dr. Melanie.

While mama had all the normal frustrations one had about their place of employment, she never took issue with treatment from Dr. Melanie because of race. They had discussions about racial inequality and about the civil rights movement. Even though mama was a struggling Black woman at the time, up against all the challenges of race tensions in the South, when it came to race, they understood each other. She respected mama and mama respected her.

My mama loved dogs and that was a thing they had in common. Dr. Melanie would come to our house to vaccinate and care for mama's dogs. They were friends, so they had friend, woman and employer disagreements. Mama wasn't too concerned about her housekeeping duties because by then, she had mastered the skill. She kept a pristine house for us as well. She trained and taught us how to cook and clean so that her home was sparkling too.

Dr. Melanie was interested in my mother's struggle. She listened and supported her when needed. Dr. Melanie received as much support from my mother as she gave. They often spent most of the day in the kitchen talking about their experiences. I remember one day going to the ranch with my mother and hearing them talk about God, raising kids and marriage. Dr. Melanie was a tough lady. She wore cowgirl Eddie Bauer well stitched pants, Cowgirl button up shirts and sturdy Frye brand boots. Frye is a brand I wear today. I like the rogue style and the look of toughness these boots give off. And they are comfortable.

Dr. Melanie was always interested in my life. She spent a lot of time teaching me, sharing books, inventive games and gadgets. She taught me how to ride and care for horses. She was the best horse doctor in the land.

Sometimes I would go with my mother to help her clean the house but would end up in the barn, vet clinic or out in the horse pasture helping Dr. Melanie deliver foals or grooming colts and phillies. It was amazing to witness her perform horse surgeries, deliveries or just simply care for the horses. The clinic cabinets were filled with pills and capsules almost as big as my hand. I went to the veterinary hospital and clinic so often, Dr. Melanie offered to pay me to keep the medical cabinets, counters and surgical tools clean and sterile. During my time at the Clinic, Dr. Melanie and I would take breaks together. She would talk and inquire of my schoolwork and try to determine if I needed anything. To this day, I think she was trying to get me to trust her. Our relationship would be long term and mutually beneficial.

Mama and Dr. Melanie created a safe space for each other. Their friendship had both trust and reverence. They became great friends. Mama would spend most of the mornings in the kitchen talking with Dr. Melanie about their trials, tribulations and triumphs. They talked about their kids and their marriage while feeding and caring for the animals on her property.

Later, Dr. Melanie invited me to go to the State-of-the-Art Veterinary Hospital. The place was immaculate. Dr. Melanie specialized in horses. She taught me about and shared her love for horses. She taught me how to ride, feed and help fold horses. I was in awe.

Dr. Melanie was a civil rights activist in my mind. Her well-polished and neat home office was lined with books about religion, history, law, race equality, Civil rights, Martin Luther King Jr. and animals. Everything you can imagine. When it was my day to dust the books shelves, I stopped to peruse the books titles and sometimes read the prefaces. Inquisitive and sometimes outright nosy, I also took note of the mail and bills on the desk. Dr. Melanie donated to many causes. From animal rights to civil rights and women's rights—Dr. Melanie used her resources to support change. She was a powerhouse. She lived her beliefs. She used her money to support people and animals who were suffering or lacking.

As someone who grew up in a small Central Florida town and was mostly exposed to the church and community life there, I was very interested in Dr. Melanie and her life at the ranch. I saw the way wealthy and privileged people lived up close and personal. I also learned how some of them care for and support the people around them. I do believe Dr. Melanie wanted me to know that she was one of the good guys.

Dr. Melanie shared with me stories of civil rights events that were taking place throughout the South at that time. She talked to me about her "save the animal" campaigns. I reveled in the books and the stories she shared. Dr. Melanie also supported me and mama when we had health issues that needed tending to. I used to think that was so funny because Dr. Melanie was a veterinarian.

One time I sprained my ankle. It was so painful. Mama took me to Dr. Melanie's veterinarians' clinic for an x-ray. Dr. Melanie said she wanted to see if it was broken before my mama spent a whole lot of money taking me to the doctor. Her x-ray showed it was broken. Mama did what she had to do to get it fixed.

My time at the ranch was gratifying. Dr. Melanie introduced me to books about traveling the world. Talking and listening to her teach me about broadening horizons was inspiring. She also encouraged me to read the *National Geographic* magazines. The magazines were piled neatly in her office. We often went on field trips with her and her children. She exposed me and my siblings to adventures we could not afford at that time. Of course, my mom took us to South Florida and some of the attractions she could afford like *Cypress Gardens* and the famous historic Silver Springs, (the colored section). I recall us taking my first trip to Tampa, Florida because the world-famous *Barnum and Bailey Circus* was coming. I loved the other attractions Florida had to offer. When I was a teenager Disney World opened. I enjoyed it immensely. This was still a segregated era, nonetheless, Dr. Melanie defended and protected us everywhere we visited.

There were oftentimes stares and discrimination in the midst. I remember when the children from a neighboring ranch came to play with Dr Melanie's kids while I was there. One of the neighbor's boys called me a Black nigger. Well, that was the last time I saw him on Dr. Melanie's property. She piled all us kids in her Cadillac, took the boy home and told his mother that he was no longer welcome at her ranch.

Dr. Melanie kept the idea of college and travel at the forefront of our conversations. She helped my mom help me through my college years. I got the idea to travel abroad in my junior year. After writing an award-winning essay I received a scholarship. Dr. Melanie presented me with the best luggage set I ever had. It was the Lark brand. Of course, I was anxious and afraid for this enormous travel opportunity. But Dr. Melanie assured me that I could handle it. Being from a small town in Florida I was not exposed to much African-American history. It was while attending my historical Black college that my mind and eyes were opened to my incredible history. Every visit home I would come with a new thing that communicated my rebellion or pride in the Black Struggle. I would visit Dr. Melanie on the ranch, and we would discuss for hours what I had learned. I was becoming a Black power student.

I learned about other religions such as Islam, Buddhism and Hinduism. I started wearing African print skirts and African head wraps. I cut my hair to a mini afro and wore the dangling copper bracelets I collected. I was not eating pork and played around with being a vegetarian. My book bag was filled with books about Malcom X and classic texts like *The Destruction of the African Civilization* by epic writer, Chancellor Williams. I also had a copy of the Quran and the famous book, *Things Fall Apart* by Chinua Achebe. My conversations with Dr. Melanie would get heated and mildly contentious during those times. She always tried to impress upon me that there were good and bad people of all races in the world. She maintained that not all White people were racist and bigoted and especially that we were all children of God. Dr. Melanie also agreed that there was evil in the world, but she strongly believed that good was greater than evil.

Dr. Melanie was a beautiful and compassionate woman. When my brother died during my second summer from college she was among my greatest supporters. I was inconsolable. I had never felt this much grief. My brother died in a car accident. He was one year older than me. One rainy summer day, weeks after the funeral, I was home in bed and could not stop crying. My Mama, experiencing her own grief, was worried about me. She was on the phone telling Dr Melanie that she thought I needed help. The next thing I knew Dr. Melanie walked in my bedroom, took off her shoes and climbed into bed with me. She held me and we both cried louder than before. She rocked me to sleep. This had nothing to do with race. I felt her sympathy and her compassion healed me.

Dr. Melanie hosted my wedding shower at her ranch. She also transported all of my wedding guests to her ranch for the bridal festivities. The ranch was decorated with apricot and white crepe paper. The flowers were roses and calla lilies.

Dr. Melanie had my bridal shower cake made at a specialty bakery. The cake was adorned with flowers and had pearls in the rose buds. She said the pearls represented wisdom. She told me that I should seek God's wisdom in everything, specially entering into marriage. When I went to cut the cake, she instructed me to cut it in a certain area. When I cut the cake, I realized she had the baker make one side of the cake chocolate and the other vanilla. She said she did this because she wanted me to always remember our discussions about race relations. And that everything is not Black and White. It was an amazing tribute to our relationship and talks over the years. Everything she did was full of wisdom and beauty.

The last time I saw Dr. Melanie, she stood up to speak at my mother's funeral amidst a sea of Black people. She was still in control. She seemed to be at home with the mourners. She spoke of my mother in a very loving way. She told the congregants that my mother was a Sister in Christ, as well as her friend and a member of her family. She told them she and my mother shared their faith with each other. She mentioned how my mother helped her raise her kids. Her daughter was there and she too shared how much she loved my mother and was honored to have my Mother stand in for her as Matron of Honor at her wedding. My mother was in her 70's when she stood up for Dr. Melanie's daughter.

Dr. Melanie finished her talk by proclaiming my mother was a prayer and faith warrior. She quoted one of my mother's favorite sayings. "God may not come when you want him but he sho' will come on time." Dr. Melanie stayed for the repast and breaking bread after the service. She hugged and kissed me and said she was slowing down. She sent me a check two weeks later with a note, "Here's a little something to take care of your travel expenses."

I celebrate the blessing of knowing this woman. She had a deep impact on who I am as a woman, wife and mother. Once again, God was preparing me for service. Her teaching me about advocacy, expansion and broad horizons and that there are good and bad people of every color was crucial to my growth. She also showed me that there is a sweetness in opening your heart to people that want to support and love you, no matter their background.

I am aware that she was in my life for a wise reason. These relationships are not unusual. There have been countless stories of fervent and caring White people helping and supporting Black people. How else would we have accomplished the strides in the Underground Railroad and the civil rights movement? Dr. Melanie was my advocate and taught me to advocate. For this I will always be grateful...

The pearls, the pearls
The words of wisdom and knowledge
Trust and be aware that the light shines
In and on the pearls.....thelma craig

Chapter 19

Brianna – Daughter in Love

Brianna had has taught me a lot and is still teaching me because she is married to my son and is the mother of my grandchildren. I regularly witness her loving the people I love. My family. She is a great addition. I thank God for placing her in my son's life.

Brianna is a strong, determined, creative and beautiful White woman. She is kind, sweet, creative and doesn't take no stuff. She came in my life about a year before she married my son. I knew I was going to like her because she started helping him pick out Christmas presents for the family before I met her. My son was doing an okay job of selecting presents and we appreciated his efforts. But when she came into his life, the presents changed and improved eloquently. They had so much meaning and usefulness. I knew she included him in the shopping time, and I also imagined that she guided him in making the choices.

The gifts were great, because they were meaningful, spiritual and profound. She helped him to choose practical and creative gifts, like bracelets for me and my daughter that had a blessed purpose. My bracelet was designed for me to have peace. I liked that.

I always told my son to pick girlfriends that cared about him for who he was. I taught him to develop his own personal relationship with God and strengthen his spiritual and mental acumen. I suggested that he choose girlfriends that were smart and that had common sense. I did tell him to pick Black girlfriends because at that time, I noticed little black girls were missing out on young Black boyfriends choosing them. All the Black boys were paired up with White girls at his school. A friend reminded me that we had chosen schools that were predominately White. Yes, we were conscious of the schools and neighborhoods we lived in and had chosen because we wanted prime educational opportunities for our children. The school district we lived in had an excellent academic record.

We also moved there because in some neighborhoods, gang violence and drugs were rampant. I soon learned that these elements were rampant everywhere but were hidden better in White neighborhoods.

I gently suggested to my son that he play with and talk to the Black girls at school. My motto at the time was, "Black girls need love too."

I did this because I was trying to raise a son who respected and loved himself and his people. My son was popular and well-liked by people of all different races. He'd always surrounded himself with culturally diverse people. We enrolled him in the Black Ski Club, the Black church Sunday School and other activities where he would be well rounded. He had friends in every color of the rainbow.

I remember when he was in elementary school, he wanted to have a party. I told him could have a party, but he had to invite Black kids from the school. He reminded me that there were only five black kids at the school. I told him I wanted all five of those Black kids at the party. They all came and so did a crew of others. It was a successful basement party!!

My son had a crush on cute little Black girl in his class in elementary school. He was grinning ear to ear when he introduced her to us. He even claimed that he loved her. She would be the first of several Black girls and women he fell hard for. All were smart and remarkable. One of the other Black mothers asked me how I had gotten my son to date Black girls. I told her that I made the suggestion because I noticed the Black girls at the school did not have Black boyfriends.

One day my son asked if he could also date brown girls. I told him yes, of course. He went on to date Latinas and a few biracial girls. After that, I let go and let him explore.

I wanted my son and daughter to be proud of their heritage and culture. I wanted them to be proud to be Black. I didn't want my son to choose a White woman because it made him feel like he had arrived or accomplished something. These are reasons why some Black men date White women. I had also heard that when a Black man dates White women its because he doesn't like his mama. I had to let all of that go because one thing I know for sure and that's that my son loves and respects me. I also know that I have cared for and nurtured him and that alone should have prepared him to love whoever he heart is led to love.

We were adamant about not allowing his small ethnic dating pool to push him into a corner. We also didn't want him to make his schoolwork a low priority. So, we pulled back on directives about how to date and focused on school. Interestingly enough, when he connected with White girls in high school, he would not bring them home to meet us.

Mind you, I was over the Black girl rule. I didn't know how to tell him that, but I sensed that he was reluctant to share who he was dating. I did tell him that I was glad he was choosing girls and relationships where there was respect and honor. When it came to relationships, my Daddy often said, "You love em' , I love em." Fortunately, he liked and respected the man that would become my husband.

When you fall in love with someone from another culture-you must love them for all they bring into your life. I have had the privilege of meeting and knowing many biracial couples. Not just Black and white, but people from different religions and sexual orientations. They have and had beautiful relationships. I do know that they will face some adversity and controversy in certain environments with prejudice, discrimination and bias because of who they chose to love. Some will straight up hate on them. I guess this isn't hard to imagine in 2018 from what we see in the media.

I raised my son and daughter to be proud of who they are and where they are from. I also enlisted the help from artists and creatives that I had in their lives. From seeing beautiful Black, African American art on the walls of our home to witnessing the beauty of our culture. This taught them to see the beauty in themselves. And I did place pictures of family throughout our home. I wanted them to see beauty in Black culture. I remember the first time my son bought home a White girl he was dating. She didn't seem to be comfortable with us. I thought it was because I was proud and impressed with my home decorum, the Afrocentric artistic surroundings. I had all kinds of Black art from Black Santa, Black Angels, African Warriors and family portraits. I also had contemporary and stylish furniture.

I may be wrong, but I had the distinct impression that she was uncomfortable in our home. I was being openhearted and welcoming. I was ready to embrace her. I knew I wasn't the cause of her discomfort, because I was as nice as pie. I made a beautiful dinner complete with pie, collard greens, black eyed peas, okra, corn bread and fried chicken. I pulled out all the stops and made a wonderful and welcoming meal.

Our kitchen and eating table were the hearth of our home. This girl still didn't seem to relax. She stood most of the time. She finally tried the collard greens.

I couldn't tell if she liked them or not. I stop worrying about it. My son seemed to like her so, I was preparing to act like I did too. That relationship didn't last long.

I thank God that my son chose a woman who would appreciate the loving family he came from. We love Brianna. She is creative in every way. She is straightforward. My father died a few months before she was to marry my son. I felt her compassion.

She really got a profound dose of love when she gave birth to my granddaughter. I knew she would be a sweet little brown girl. And she is. She would have the curls and beauty of a beautiful African American princess. I adore her essence. She is a combination of a White mother and her Black father, my son. I also admire how Brianna loves her baby's hair and complexion.

If someone asked me what the good qualities are you want to see in a woman that marries your son, I would have much to say but not too much. Because this question is best answered by my son when he chooses a partner. But I can say that the woman my son chose is all that and more. My favorite is her thoughtfulness, compassion and dependability. I will never forget an incident after my father's death. I came back home after a week of funeral arrangements and settling the estate. I had just spent weeks nursing my Daddy, holding his hand and standing in the gap as he passed. What an experience.

I was more than burnt out. I was spiritually, mentally and physically exhausted. I flew home to Colorado days later in sheer exhaustion. I fell asleep on the ride to the house. When I arrived home and walked into my kitchen, there were meals placed on the stove and counter that was meant to sustain me for about a week. There was a pot of Jambalaya, Rice, Baked Chicken Wings, Salad fixings and a chocolate cake. She knows I like chocolate, so she often prepares me a homemade chocolate desert. Brianna is thoughtful, considerate and mindful. She notices things that you desire or yearn for and tries her best to get it for you. She recognized that I like tea. She made sure I had my very own teacup with an assortment of exotic teas.

It not the material things she buys, it's her thoughtfulness. I love her because she seems to bless our family in so many ways. She fits in well. She engages and genuinely laughs at our family jokes. She gets it. She enjoys our family traditions and meals.

I love the way she loves her baby's skin and hair. She is a great mommy. Her little brown baby looks at her with nothing but love. Because she sees her for who she is. I do too. And it is a beautiful thing to see her love her brown babies. Why not--love is love. When she married my son, she had to have known that he is from a proud and noble family. We are who we are, and I know she knows it. You cannot marry into a family and not embrace the history and culture of the one you married. It is imperative to appreciate where your wife or husband comes from and who they are totally.

So, I really like having her in my life. She is a gift to our family. She is a great mother to my grandchildren. She is a help blessing to my son.

See how we grow and shift the narrative? We gain understanding in love. With the tension of race relations in this country today, I am grateful that I still have a heart. My relationship with women from different backgrounds has been amazing. I have encountered evil and ignorance. But recognizing the good in the hearts of others without prejudice and judgement is a graceful part of being a woman. God continues to put me on the path of goodness, and I refuse to let racism taint my purpose in life. To women who cherish their daughter in laws, I say more power to you. Love—love will conquer all!

I learned that you cannot chose a partner for your son or daughter. Also, they truly are in the hands of God. They came through us as their parents but once born, they are here in God's hands. And God has ordered their path. All we can do is pray the same way our parents did and ask God to cover them with that hedge of protection. Pray that they make the right decisions and seek God for direction and guidance. My Daddy and Mama told me that they prayed for me. They prayed for all their Grandchildren. Their prayer was that we be protected and delivered from evil.

They prayed that we did not make choices that if wrong, could not be repaired. Because parents know their children will make mistakes and fall short sometimes. My husband and I pray this and more. We pray that our children, grandchildren and great grandchildren will be blessed with people in their lives who love them as much as we do. If God is who He says He is and gives us what He has promised, they will be just fine. So, I am grateful for having a daughter-in-law that loves like she does. She is a woman of God.

I see you, you see me

We see together
We are in this together
and we have so much to share
Gather the moment, the times,
*the blessings to share…..***thelma craig**

Chapter 20
Miss Potts – Saving Grace

Sensitive to the ways in which my schoolmates attacked me every day, my second-grade teacher, Miss Potts, was a Godsend. They called me everything except a child of God. Blacky, tar baby, midnight, ugly black. I will not capitalize these names while I'm writing. These names were just a few of the names they called me on a constant basis. It happened in the classroom, in the lunchroom, on the playground and at church. They had it in for me. The amazing thing is that most of my classmate's skin was dark or darker than mine. I could never understand that. Still don't. If it was not for my brother and my Daddy throwing a life buoy out to me during those times, I would have drowned in the sea of peer pressure. I thought my dark skin was the only object of their assaults.

My brother, who was a year and a half year older, scolded me, "It was because you allowed them to say and do that."

He always told me that it was not because of my skin color that they picked on me. It was because I was smart and cute. They didn't want me to be all that.

"Maybe they couldn't understand why you were so dark, cute and smart. They only tease you because they see that it bothers you and they want you to feel bad about yourself, so you won't do your work in school. Don't let them see that it gets to you," My brother used to say.

Miss Potts was the one who would watch over and protect me from the tirade that ensued before, during and after class whenever she could. I was a nervous wreck. I feared the time Miss Potts would leave the class. I really wanted the tormenting to stop. I loved going to school. I loved my teachers, the books, the playtime games and lunchtime. I continued to hold the record in the local Spelling Bee.

Miss Potts was very beautiful light skinned woman. She could almost pass for a White woman. She had traveled the world. She tried to teach us how to use chop sticks. She shared stories of her travels. The reason I love maps and globes today is because Miss Potts had many globes and maps all over her classroom. She loved to talk about history and faraway places.

Miss Potts was also an activist. I recall often my Daddy and Mama saying that Miss Potts was a powerful woman in our town. She attended rallies, marches and protests. She introduced new ways of thinking to our community.

An innovator and trailblazer, Miss Potts was the teacher that introduced a "new math" to our segregated elementary school in central Florida. Our schools were given old books and secondhand books and curriculums. Even though we had compassionate and great teachers, they were forced to teach us in a racist society that did not provide the new books or updated curriculums to our district. Our teachers had to fight to give us an education equal to our White counterparts while still trying to give the students love and care. Thinking back, it was Miss Potts who taught us Algebra and Trigonometry. Our school was being introduced to this math on a small scale much later than the White schools.

Miss Potts paid close attention to all of her students. She knew if they were sad or happy when they entered her class. She always gave you a once overlook when you walked in. I can still remember her stare and feeling her care after she had rescued me from bullying classmates. She would physically remove me and talk to me about how I was feeling. She would genuinely ask, "How you doing today?"

Long story short, Miss Potts was the teacher that took my mother aside and said, "She can't continue to come to school day in and day out and be subjected to this taunting amongst her classmates. They pick on her all the time."

She recommended that my mom take me to an all-White elementary school called College Park. It was on the outskirts of the Black neighborhood. Fortunately, the school was on my mama's way to work in the rural part of town. This town and predominantly White community was known for its sprawling ranches and horse farms. Miss Potts reasoning was that my White peers would receive me in wonder because I was different. Very different from them. She told my mama that I would have access to more opportunities. She was right.

That's when I started learning how to play the clarinet and read music. We did not have instruments and instrumental music at the colored school. We had music in the form of singing. My mama didn't hesitate to follow Miss Potts' instructions and she proved to be right.

I had a safe and uneventful transition all the way through elementary school. I had a reprieve from kids constantly picking on me. I was going to the third grade. I arrived without event. The teacher introduced me to the class and they all said their names.

The only thing I remember that was slightly dubious is when a little White boy named Donny who had blonde, shoulder-length hair, stood next to me in the lunch line. He put his arm around me at the shoulder. I put my arm around his shoulder.

Pensive and careful he asked, "Thelma, why is your hair so stiff?"

I knew what he meant. Because my ponytails were pressed, greased and parted exceptionally that day, my hair didn't move even when the wind blew.

I looked and him and shrugged, "I don't know, Donny. Why is your hair so shaky?"

He said he didn't know. We both shrugged and moved up in the lunch line, grabbed our lunch trays and sat down together with the other kids. There would be no mention of my hair or my skin color from that day on through my third-grade school year. From then on, I never had my skin color mentioned and I was never the subject of bullying.

I think Miss Potts knew that I needed this freedom from my own people to breathe. She told my mother that if I didn't change or transfer to another school, I would not be able to study and

maintain academically. Sadly, I had to attend an all-White school to be safe from bullying. For some reason, even with the issues of segregation at that time, my mother didn't have trouble enrolling me. I'm sure Miss Potts had something to do with that.
I not only survived I thrived at the new school. Then I had to move to another school the next year because of my mom and Daddy's separation. We moved in with my grandma in South Florida for a year.   I went back to the colored school in sixth grade. I was stronger by then and more confident and was able to navigate through my final year of elementary school.

I never forgot about Miss Potts. I keep her in my heart and mind. I am grateful for her understanding of African American history. It was because she understood how we were treated as Black people that she understood how we treated each other.
Some Blacks take pride themselves in denigrating someone who is darker than them. This was because they did not and do not understand the power and beauty of melanin rich skin.

Miss Posts protected me the best way she knew how. Now that I think about it, I would guess Miss Potts empathized with me because she was ridiculed for being extremely light skinned. I would learn later that light skinned Black people are equally taunted.
I would also learn the song that was used to taunt people with dark skin.
Black get back. Brown stick around. White, you alright!

Miss Potts wasn't married but she was wedded to the salvation of her students by any means necessary. How innovative was it of her to suggest I be removed from my home school—an all-Black environment and put in an all-White setting. She had powerful insight and wisdom to determine what my battered soul needed at that time. And I thank God for positioning her in my path. Miss Potts was an unsung Shero in the Civil rights fight. I will never forget the lift, the breath and the chance to be free at least for a moment.

Thank you, Miss Potts for being an advocate for our people and for providing an above and beyond education to me and other children. Thank you for recognizing that I needed a break and an environment where a smart, beautiful, Black skinned girl could thrive. We need teachers in our life who values the whole child educational experience. I understand now that this teacher was offering culturally competent learning for me.

Mark my words, you are great
Mark my words, you are light
Mark my words and take this chance for blessing on your journey
*You are walking in the path of immensity, you are worthy…..**thelma craig***

Chapter 21
Emma – My Courage

My husband and I moved into our third home on the quest to find the right neighborhood to live and raise our kids. We were a young couple that had moved thousands of miles away from our families. I always had an array of family members in my immediate environment. Being this far away from them made us extremely protective and watchful of where we lived. My husband had always wanted to go west. So after a year of marriage we trekked west. There were no grandmas, granddaddies, no aunts, uncles or cousins close by. Yet, God placed many people in our path that made us feel welcome and safe and encouraged.

A powerful, tough-love woman lived just across the street from us when my daughter was six years old and my son was about three and a half. This was the second house we owned. Our neighbor, Emma and her husband had two young boys around the same age as our kids. We had gone through a number of daycares and babysitters by the time I met Emma. We got to know her family and she offered to babysit my young son because he was not in elementary school yet and neither was her youngest son.

Oh, what a blessing this was! I immediately felt at home and trusted Emma. She reminded me of all my Aunts and great Aunts rolled into one. She would invite me over for a cocktail after work. Emma was a stay home mom and housewife. And she was very devoted to her family. We established a relaxing relationship. Always laughing and talking about our lives. Cocktails sometimes put us in a relaxed state of being and enhanced our ability to share and be vulnerable. Amazing, Yet I know I know that prayer, meditation, yoga and mindfulness practice enhances your peacefulness to engage in an enlightening conversation. But I welcomed the cocktail.

Emma was real. She had no airs of pretense. She told it like it was. She came from a tough and challenging background in the Midwest. But she always talked about how she was always surrounded by love. Her survival stories blessed and impressed me. She was married to a devoted man. She shared with me that even though her family had hard times, love always carried them through. I let go and trusted her. Our relationship thrived.

Emma made a profound impression on my son because she was a tough love mother. She talked to all the kids like she meant business. She also let them know that they were valuable and cared for. Emma made certain that they had all the current toys, video games, books and a library card. She helped them with their homework. She was intent on raising confident, strong, Black men. That was her mantra. The kids were kept clean, neat and free of stuffy, runny noses. She kissed and hugged them robustly daily. She used profanity in a non-threatening way. She pointed in their face and encouraged them to look her in the eye and challenge her if they needed to. She was not abusive with her language that was just her way of communicating. She grew up around old school hipsters. I'll admit to having a little concern that because Emma used profanity, my little son would become a potty mouth. I never heard him curse around me during the time he was being cared for by Emma. It was many years later when he was a senior in high school that I heard him cursing with his teammates. He was Captain of the football team. I understand that boys will be boys in the privacy of their male circles.

Emma and I continued to enjoy our cocktails and talked late into the night. I was compelled to be vulnerable and open in our discussions. She did most of the talking telling me about her life and experiences using a curse word every other word. Shit, goddamamnit was among them but the "F" word was her favorite. Somehow, it did not sound profane or offensive to me. It's not like I didn't have relatives that cursed around me during my childhood. Usually, she was engrossed in telling me her stories when the language spewed from her mouth. It was mostly humorous. She was passionate about her life experiences. She took the edge off the distress in the situation.

There is something about having friends in your life that is older than you are. Emma is/was about twelve years older than me. She looked great for her age. Slim trim and always chic. Her hair was always fried, dyed and laid to the side. Yet she took care of young kids and I swear they were her reason for living and thriving. She was an enforcer. Her straight shooting and tough love persona were the ultimate gift. She encouraged and demanded that the kids she cared for read, listened, obeyed and played hard. She demanded respect and she also gave it.

Even if she was cursing their "little asses" out for leaving their plate on the table after lunch. It was like she knew how to get the best and the truth from them. She knew how to get the best and truth out of me too. When Emma questioned me, she was serious and penetrating. She also would curse me out—lovingly of course—if I wasn't open and forthright.

She asked me one day, "Now that you a grown woman and raising your own babies, how do you feel about your mother?"

Emma and her questions often caught my spirit and mind off guard. I thought for a minute, looked her in the eye and admitted that I loved my mother, but I did have some concerns about her ways of raising me. I explained how I did not feel she protected me enough when I was being attacked and harassed for being a dark-skinned girl. I am sure she heard the names and knew about the taunting. You see my mother had a light complexion. I thought if I was her complexion, they wouldn't tease me. I didn't think it mattered to her. I often thought back and surmised that she didn't know how hard it was for me to be bullied and attacked for being a dark-skinned little girl, because she had light skin.

After that talk with Emma I realized I had some unresolved issues with my mother. Emma told me like it was once again.

"You're a grown woman now and you must look at it and let it go. Tell your mom how you felt and release it. She did the best she could. You turned out to be healthy and whole. But you need to share that with your mother. Tell her how you felt as a child and thank her for raising you to be a good person. After her response, tell her that you appreciate her struggles with raising you on your own after her and your father divorced."

This time she was physical and profound in her gesture.

She got out of her seat, moved toward me in a swift motion, placed her hand on my back and said "Get up and get your ass home and call your mother. You shouldn't waste another minute not talking to your mother about what's unresolved. She old enough to understand and appreciate your honesty. Get your ass up and call your mother, dammit."

I could feel her eyes on my back as I walked across the street to my house. She yelled at me, "You had better call her! I can see you from the window. Let me see you do it. Call, dammit!"

I entered the house and ran upstairs to our room. I picked up the phone from the side of the bed and moved the curtains back wide. I peered across the street, there Emma was still standing in her front door with her hands on her hip and pointing a finger toward me. I called my mom. I forgot about the two-hour time difference. I knew she was probably winding down from the day and getting ready for bed. I asked how her day went, how she was feeling. I told her I was just thinking lately about when I was growing up. How I didn't feel she protected me enough when kids attacked me because I was dark skinned.

Mama didn't skip a beat in responding.

"Baby, I think about that all the time too. Now that you are a grown, beautiful Black woman, I hoped it didn't bother you anymore. I know how much trouble you had with that. And all I can say is I wished I could have protected you more. You were the prettiest little thing. I knew you were teased but I didn't know what to do. I just prayed it would not cause you too much harm. So, baby, please forgive mama. I did the best I could."

I levitated. That was a great moment. Then she went on ask me about my husband and the kids. I was grateful and still excited. I welcomed the next subjects in our conversation. I was happy and content with her apology and explanation.

Needless to say, Emma was proud of me. We shared many other conversations about life. That was a passage in my life where I felt safe to explore more about my unhealed issues. About how we can't let the childhood nuisances keep us back. Emma believed that if we recall them, embrace them and move on, we can heal. Emma also emphasized how we need to also recognize the great and blessed moments in our past. She used to say, "It wasn't all bad. Look at the goodness you were given."

Emma confirmed that our past shaped us. This was yet another confirmation for me that if we harbor resentment toward the people in our childhoods, it steals our Joy. I understand in the by and by that, you must examine, embrace then release the issues and concerns. It is often a misunderstanding. I did reach out to a therapist once to help me understand these issues. But it is nothing like talking to a wise sister friend.

Emma always told me how much she liked her damn self and how the experiences she had made her who she was. She talked about the fierce love she had for her mother. She said that our mothers came up in an era where it was not as easy raising kids. She said they did the best they could which is exactly what my mama said. It was even harder raising kids when you were divorced from their Daddies. And she said they didn't have many outlets or safe spaces to look at it, must less talk about it.

Eventually, my mama and I had very deep conversations. Healing conversations. But usually it was about other people's pain and God, The Lord as she called Him. I was grateful for Emma that day. Insisting that I have a conversation with my mama about that one thing I was holding on to. Mama was too.

I recall a very powerful morsel my mom gave to me as a young adult. It was a day or so after my wedding, as I was leaving for the honeymoon she whispered, "Remember Sista, you can always come home." That let me know I was safe and that I didn't ever have to feel alone trapped in a marriage or any other situation.

It was after my experience and time with Emma in my life that I began cataloguing the good messages I received from the women in my life. I am understanding better by and by.

Tap, Tap, Tap into my heart
Pierce your lessons and your guidance
Loving ways into the spheres of my ears
Hearing and knowing the path to
*womanhood.....***thelma craig**

Chapter 22
Isabelle – Laughter and Adventure

Isabelle was an outstanding character to add to my experience and journey to understanding and appreciating why some were in my path. What a spirited woman! There was something about her that I liked from the first time we met. I didn't know exactly what it was. Isabelle was in my life for a brief moment. I have not seen her since. She was like the wind. She blew through like a fresh breeze. I met her on the Job. She was an outstanding co-worker. She always made it fun to come to work because of her fun-loving humorousness. The great work ethic she demonstrated taught me a lot about how to love and serve people.

Isabelle was a neat Italian girl with beautiful olive skin and short black hair. She was sharp in every way, always thinking on her feet. That sharpness attributed to her zest for life. She loved kids and loved to have fun. Her motherhood skills never ceased to amaze me. She doted on her girls. They were two lively, friendly children and had that same zest for living as their mother.

It is good to stop and appreciate the qualities in others. It helps you sharpen and appreciate your own good qualities. Isabelle gave me so much in such a short span of time. I do hope I had an impact on her. My fear of authority was tested and bought forth with her shenanigans.

This was the year when the media was overwhelmed with the news of Aurora Police Officer's unfairness and brutality, with African American citizens. I had started to subconsciously feel fear for my life when I was in the presence of a policeman. That year I had been stopped in traffic on two different occasions by rude and nasty policemen. I became paranoid and full of anxiety while driving. It was always times when I was on my way to work. I would arrive to work a nervous wreck. After I dropped off my baby at the day care, I drove stoically and slowly to work.

When I arrived, Isabelle looked at her watch and mouthed, "You late. What's up?" She would then greet me with a smile. I knew she knew that I'd had a bad experience on the way to work.

On one particular day driving to work, I barely paused at a stop sign. I traveled that intersection daily but didn't remember seeing a stop sign there. The next thing I knew an Aurora policeman appeared behind me with flashing lights. I stopped. He got out of his cruiser and walked toward me with his hand on his gun.

"You know you just ran through a stop sign," He barked while looking in the back seat of the car where my baby slept.

I said nothing. He asked for my registration and license. His eyes were on me. His hand was still on his gun. I was terrified. I gave the documents to him. He barked, "Wait here."

He went back to his cruiser and checked my information in the system. It was fifteen of the longest minutes in my life. I sweated so hard my entire collar was drenched.

He returned. He threw the document in the car and said, "If you didn't have that damn baby in the back seat, I'd run your ass in."

I could not speak. Through my watered eyes, I tried to read the name on his badge. He returned to his cruiser and drove off speedily.

I just sat there for a few minutes. After I composed myself, I drove off. When I arrived at work, Isabelle noticed my appearance and mood. She motioned me to the door and we went into the ladies room where I shared my ordeal. I cried and she consoled me. She talked and talked. She tried to make a joke about it to get me to laugh it off. I did wonder how she could understand the fear and terror I experienced at the hands of a police officer. She was a white woman.

Weeks went by. My birthday was approaching. I always get excited about my birthday. Isabelle called on Saturday. "Hey, I have to run a few errands and I need you to go to Target with me."

I said ", okay". An hour or so later, I hopped in her hot red convertible Volkswagen.

When we arrived at Target she said, "I need you to take my credit card, go into Target and get the two items on this note. Use my card. I'm going to run to another store."

I was wide mouthed and shocked. "I can't use your credit card. "That's illegal."
She brushed me off and said, "It's not a problem. Just get the items and sign for them with my credit card." After almost an hour, she persuaded me to go in. I went into Target, purchased the items and paid for them with her card, signing her name. I was so afraid. She was waiting for me outside. She assured me that everything was ok. She laughed and we never mentioned the event again.

My birthday arrived. I was in my cubicle working away, smiling happily because it was my birthday. I knew I would spend a lovely evening with my family after work. I looked up because there was a commotion in the aisle of the cubicle. I peeked out and saw a Police Officer standing tall in the entry area.

He said, "Is there a Thelma Craig here?" I stood and entered the aisle.

Trembling and walking cautiously. I said, "I'm Thelma Craig."

He approached me and said, "Are you the Thelma Craig that uses other peoples' credit cards. I was stunned and confused. I thought about Isabelle. He began to handcuff me. I resisted with a shrug and stated, "I didn't do anything wrong."
My supervisor stood by and placed her hand on my shoulders.

I said, "Wait a minute, he can't arrest or handcuff me before reading me my rights."
Tears were flowing now. My supervisor approached me with a concerned look on her face.

She told the officer, "You are welcome to go in my office and talk about this."

The policeman took me into my supervisor's office. In close proximity, my co-workers were standing by whispering and giggling.

The officer handcuffed me to the chair. Then the music started to play. Then the policeman started to dance and remove his tie. I then realized he was a stripper. This was supposed to be a birthday party. I don't think I felt relief until I got home for the evening. It was quite a day.

I guess Isabelle came to remind me of a quality in myself that I had always liked, spontaneity. To live in the moment. Don't be too serious. But in that moment, I preferred a nice planned event.

I also recognized the impact of racism on our mental health and overall safety. In today's society and the society in which we have lived since the slave trade, Black people have been subject to racist actions. We have endured meanness, brutality and discrimination only because of the color of our skin. Providing the notion and oftentimes the reality that the justice and police system is not always fair to us. This causes some of us to live in fear of the bias embedded in the system.

Isabelle was so proud of herself. Her surprise made me want to release my bowels during the time it was happening. Having Isabelle breeze through my life at that time gave me a glimpse of the fear many Blacks live with every day, up close and personal. It was a practical joke, but it made me realize how even minor incidents with the police effect me and so many others. I had some work to do. I needed healing. My anxiety about race relations had to be addressed.

These days, I try to recognize my fear when it appears. Isabelle often said I take myself to seriously. That may be so, but I'm learning to let go and trust God.

I did begin to think the practical joke was funny after a few days passed. I often think of that fear though. Isabelle had a great sense of humor. But she did not understand my deep fears about law enforcement. We may have had a lot in common on a sense of humor level. But I don't think she could ever know what that feels like. She was funny, exciting and we shared lots of other good times. All in the name of fun and adventure.

Because this soul issue was brought up in me, I was able to examine my reactions when adverse racial issues take place. I also learned to be resilient in the face of racism. I must do this work. Especially, if I am to raise Black children, serve others and become a healthy productive woman in this society.

"We are either walking in the direction of love or the direction of fear."~ Marianne Williamson.

Funny how it rains,
Silly how it pours,
Sunshine in our hearts
Smiles on us......thelma craig

Chapter 23
Daughter –
My Teacher

It seemed as though the mamas came to rescue and comfort me while I was expecting and about to give birth to my baby girl. My mama made plans to arrive on my due date. She planned to stay for two weeks to help us with being new parents. Lord knows I didn't know what to do in those early days.

My mother-in-love was coming two weeks after the baby was due. I was scared and welcomed all the support I could get. This was my first baby. A girl. All babies—no matter the sibling position or timing—are special. But I got the feeling that my mama was celebrating my first child to the utmost. During her visit, my mama told me stories about my childhood and her experience giving birth to me. She told me what time I was born and what she thought about when I arrived. Then she went into sharing her wisdom about raising a girl child.

"You have to be patient with a daughter."

"I found myself wanting my daughter to be greater and have a better life than me."

Mama said, "You always want your children's life to be better. You'll understand by and by."

Mama inspected and observed our household. She also took note of my wifely duties and observed how my husband treated me. I could tell she was pleased. However, she did have something to say about me not ironing and preparing my husbands' clothes for work.

"He was ironing his clothes before he met me." She accepted my reason for not doing what she saw as a wife's duty.

My mama's sense of humor soared when she was around my husband. He still reminisces about the funny conversations they had. She waited and waited with us. She even suggested remedies for the baby to hurry up and come, like taking me on a drive on bumpy roads. We did it. She suggested that I eat lots of vegetables, like collard greens, green beans and even prunes! We did that. None of it worked.

I was two weeks late. My husband's mother arrived the same day my mother was leaving on the train. They were happy to see each other and be a part of a momentous occasion. I always admired how they liked and respected each other.

My daughter was going to have it her way, in her own time. She made us wait a little while longer. I was all up in my feelings. I was about to be a mama. I was fearful and anxious but feeling blessed. Both of our mothers had spoken about how waiting for the baby to come teaches us patience.

"Must be something she is gifted to teach you." And they just laughed.

Meanwhile, I grew more impatient. My mother-in-love spent her time telling me about having daughters. She and I talked well into the night. She had raised seven boys and two girls so I knew she knew what she was talking about.

"You have to be real patient with daughters.

The pressure will be on. You must be careful not to want them to be just like you because you are a female. Let them be themselves. Oh, Thelma. You will be alright. Just you wait and see."

Those were pivotal moments in my life. Moments that brought an even more special meaning to having a daughter.

My mother-in-love also bought me an interesting gift. It was wrapped really nice, in pink of course (just like the box of pink lace dresses she sent after the baby was born).

The pink package included HOUSE dresses! *House Dresses.* The kind of dresses mothers, grandmas and aunties wear around the house as they went about their daily piddling. The kind of dresses they wear when they are doing things like shelling peas, cooking, cleaning and taking care of all the children. For some reason, I didn't like the memory of the house dresses. I remembered how women would wash and wear them so much that they started tearing at the seams. But I tell you those dresses were so very comfortable, and they came in handy after I had the baby. It was easy to breastfeed in them. As I matured in my womanhood, I realized the beauty and the comfort of those dresses. I wear house dresses around the house now but I try to make sure they are cute, clean and sexy. I chose sexy house dresses because my husband does pay attention to how I keep myself together. Most importantly, I make sure the dresses are comfortable. What I really like is that you can walk around in them without wearing a bra!

I look back on those moments spent with the mamas and cherish the blessings they gave me offering comfort, support and love. I was blessed by them as they waited to welcome my daughter. Baby Girl came the next day after my mother-in-law left. Bright and early in the morning, I felt the cramps. This was the day the doctors said they would induce labor because she was so late. She was not late. I realized later that she was right on time, her time, my time and God's time. She has taught me a little more of the patience that God wants me to have. My husband and his parents made light of the fact that she came in her own time and the time is right. And now I see that patience is a virtue and my daughter continue to teach me that.

Giving birth to my daughter was quite the experience. I really threw a tantrum when the doctor told me that the baby was breech. From a logical perspective, I knew what breech meant, but the thought of it scared the shit out of me. Instead of me waiting and talking with the doctor and my husband about it and finding out the next steps, I went off. I was dramatic and acted as impatient as I could. You would have thought they told me the baby was dead. Once they finally calmed me down, I realized I had really overreacted. I thought about what our mothers said about my daughter coming here to teach us patience. I imagined my baby girl upside down in my womb thinking, *God sent me here to teach her patience. If she can just hold on, she's going to be really blessed.*

I was worried there was going to be trouble with the delivery. Again, I had to remember to be patient. I reminded myself, *God got this.*

Our baby girl arrived healthy and beautiful. I was present and alert when she arrived because of my sweet anesthesiologist. I believe he flirted with me as he administered the anesthesia. And that kept me calm and made me chuckle inside.

My daughter was the most beautiful, cocoa puff, I had ever seen. I was in celebration on the surgery table.

The doctors and the nurses cheered after I told them her name. It was like a party in the operating room.

"Yay Amber!""

I named her after my Daddy whose names was Ambers. I so dearly loved that name. I smile every time I call her name.

The birth of my daughter was one of my best celebrations. After they closed me up, they examined my daughter and handed her to me. I was amazed to be a mama.

I thank God for the doctor who helped me give birth. He was an on-call doctor and was not only highly skilled, he had a great bedside manner. He made the experience less scary. He was kind, gentle and kind of handsome for a White man. He was white—I mean so white it looked like he wore white powder. But he had a demeanor and Spirit like no other doctor I have encountered. He calmed my historical racial fears. Because of racism, I had always chosen female doctors of color. The doctor came to see me hours after the surgery.

He lifted my cocoa baby up in his arms, held her close to his chest and said, "You sure know how to make a baby."

He reminded me of how I acted before the delivery and advised me that all I had to do was relax and be patient.

"God blessed you with the most beautiful baby I have ever held."

I beamed and said, "You're right."

I get grateful every time I think about how much my daughter means to me. The beautiful, wonderment of having a daughter. I also remember the lesson about being patient. My daughter arrived after her due date and through her lateness taught me how to be patient. She came into the world on her and God's time. She is that way to this day. I admire the fact that she takes her time and think things through. I also admire how she stops to explain little things to her daughter. She is very patient and that is a good trait for a parent to have.

When my daughter was little, I used to get frustrated with the relaxed way she did things. She did her chores at a very slow pace. She didn't answer my questions fast enough. All trivial stuff, now it seems. She wasn't going or getting it like I wanted her to fast enough. She would not turn her homework in on time. Come to find out that the homework was done, complete and excellent. She just wasn't ready to turn the work in. I was certain she wouldn't finish school on time. But my daughter succeeded and finished in the right time. She just took her time letting it all sink in.

God prevailed. My daughter was smart. Yet she was thoughtful and did turn in her work when it was her time. I had to learn to accept that. I had to learn that your daughter is not you. She does things in her own time.

I encouraged my daughter to read the books I collected on the shelf. I was giving her wisdom without even thinking about it. We have had some great conversations about becoming a woman. I made sure she had access to the books I read, the people I knew and my thoughts. I shared with her as best I could. She shares her wisdom gracefully. My daughter is wise. She inherited that wisdom from my mama, my grandma and my great grand mama as far as I can see. I listen to her sometimes and think WOW, she has such insight.

Don't get it twisted—my daughter was a handful when she hit puberty. She tested my deep core. WE survived. I tried to impart wisdom by experiences. I reluctantly became a Girl Scout Leader for ten years. I wanted to share community service with her. I wanted her to get a different side of being a Scout.

I remember the lessons they taught me. At that time, I figured they only celebrated White women. I was a brownie to a lost interest. I didn't care. I had many years and stages in a girl's life to develop the activities and experience all the girls were having as Scouts. I wanted to share in this experience with my daughter in a way that I didn't have on my experience as a girl scout. I wanted to broaden her horizons. I wanted to introduce her to pioneer trailblazing Black women. While I was teaching, I was checking out teachers. My daughter is my teacher even to this day.

I can share many instances where I had to back up off my daughter while she learned. I recall one time waiting for her to explode, be a daring teenager. I was impatient. Because I read somewhere that you should expect your child to rebel or be diligent in their teenage years. You have to work it out because you don't want to have to deal with them acting out too much as young adults. I waited and waited. Well, she exhibited a small amount of rebelliousness by not turning in her work and talking back with the smart mouth quick witness. Nothing major happened until she hijacked the car (with having no license or drivers training) when her Daddy and I were out on date night. We came home and noticed the other car was missing in the garage. All I could think was that, *she finally did it*! She did something outside of the norm. I believed that kids should at least act out as teenagers, so they don't act out too much as adults

And what a teacher she is, a *real* teacher my daughter is. She taught me to see myself. I tried to give her all the good in me.

My daughter told me about an experience she had as an adult teaching elementary school. A student, a Black girl, was crying and throwing an all-out tantrum. The incident occurred in the hallway. The little girl would not respond to the consoling and touch of others. When my daughter approached her, she touched her and looked her in the eyes and said, "Hey b, you little beauty. What's up?" The girl calmed, looked her in the eye, then eyed her all over. She was teary-eyed but her face broke into a minor smile.

My daughter, because of who she was, calmed the whole situation down. Not only by telling her she was beautiful but by showing her through her own reflection. My daughter has a way with kids. She has patience with them. She said all it took was a touch and a presence. My daughter always made fun of me and of an ole' Southern Girl thing that I do. I touch. When I'm trying to make a point in exclamation or consultation, I touch. When I'm excited I touch hard. That's what makes them laugh. I think she inherited the touch from me without knowing it. She touches.

We don't always see eye to with the choices she makes in her life, yet she knows we love her. We pray that whatever decision she make, she will make and learn in her own time. We also pray that the choices she makes don't harm her irreparably.
Her father and I are always praying that our children and grandchildren live with the protection of God over their lives. We also know and heard our parents and grandparent's prayed that same prayer for us. They prayed for a hedge of protection. I pray that prayer for my daughter.

The hardest thing to accept and be patient with was that their lives are not in our control. God has control. They came through us to prepare them. They came to us to teach us that God will hold Her children in the palm of His hand.

We learned that when we get discouraged, be patient. I was so anxious and pregnant with impatience when I was carrying my daughter. I used to cry myself to sleep. I wanted the experience to be over. And when It was over, my blessing was the gift of my daughter. And that is how I learned that in those moments where we are immensely impatient, just wait. God has a beautiful plan. At the end of my waiting time, I was able to hold my beautiful daughter.
I remember when the Doctor confirmed I was pregnant. I was so excited. I kept saying, "I am going to be a mother. I'm going to be a mother." I had to sit with that and reflect on what it really meant to become a mama.

I have to admit I'm still fascinated by the role. I know there will be even greater revelations about being a mother and grandmother. Being a mother taught me that I was here to learn from another being. I also had to show her the way certain things should be done. And then I went back to waiting, waiting for more blessings in being her mama. And the blessings continue to come. She makes me proud.

I was going to cry today, Lord God
Then I thought about it
It is a necessity, you know, crying and waiting on God
But you have no reason to cry today, though
Because I am blessed with a beautiful daughter
Just breathe
I did anyhow.....thelma craig

Chapter 24
Pauline- Twins

I didn't want to say too much, but I had to say something about her. She mirrored some great qualities in me. I guess you could say we were a lot alike. It was hard for me to see at first. Especially during disagreements. Sometimes things are just hard to describe. This woman impacted my life in very close, private ways. And for giving me those qualities I appreciate her more. I am very grateful that Pauline showed up in my life.

Pauline was similar but different than me. She reminded me of my mama. She is smart, witty, tough and closed. She was born the day before my mother's birthday. They had the same temperament. My mama had a heart of gold, but you wouldn't know it right away. Same as Pauline.

We have been friends for a long time. I have always wanted and hoped for a friend I could share my innermost thoughts with, without judgment. A person that saw the best and the worst in me and didn't judge. A friend that has your best interest at heart. A friend who cherishes your hopes and dreams and wants to support you in that.

I value hanging out with smart people. I am not jealous of the best qualities in women. I appreciate and admire them. I'm always wondering how can they teach me to do that? I would hope that they would appreciate the good in me. A person who cries when you cry. Someone who celebrates when you celebrate.

You like and love each other for who you are and where you are. Someone whose often thinks and feels the same way you do.

I remember meeting my husband's grandfather before our marriage. Upon meeting me the first time, Grandpa did predict that I would marry his grandson. I was best friends with my husband's brother at the time. It probably confused his grandfather's psychic intuition. He said, "I can't put my finger on it just yet', but you're going to marry one of these here boys." I laughed it off with my two friends. Well, during that visit, before his 6:30pm bedtime, he shared a story with us. His wife, who we called Grandma, was anxious for him to turn in for bed. She couldn't hardly get a word in edge wise when he had the floor. She was so sweet and respectful—she allowed him to talk to his grandkids first.

He told us this story. "There was this woman that always hung out with this other woman. If you saw this woman, the other woman would be there. They would go to the store together. They went to the club together. They were seen as real tight. One day, something happened to the other woman. People asked her if she heard about the incident involving her friend. She said no, I don't know who you're talking about. They said, "We saw you at the club and at the store with this woman."
The woman answered, "Just because we were at the club together doesn't mean she was my friend."

They got indignant. " We saw you walking together."

And she replied, "Just because you saw us walking together, doesn't mean she was my friend." They were puzzled and said, "But we saw you with her several times at the party." The woman said, "Yeah, but she was not my friend. Yes, you saw us together. We went here and there. We went shopping together. But we never *cried* together."

I took this to mean that you can love all your associates and friends but there are some that are the true meaning of friend. The ones you can cry tears of joy with and those who you can share your pain with. Grandpa's story took me back to the memory of my friend Pauline.

I always thought I was a smart person. I had academic acumen and I had common sense. I don't know if I mentioned earlier that I won spelling bees in first grade. Even though I was battered by my peers in school, I still managed to do my homework and pay attention in class. I loved reading and enjoyed every aspect of learning. I was studious. When I was in college, I thrived and survived. Yet, I was shy about accomplishing my goals in the academic arena. In Pauline, I met my match. Pauline is and was really smart. She was analytical, studious, ambitious and just downright knew how to shine. She was an Ivy League student. I was both impressed and proud of my friend's numerous accomplishments.

Our journey to settling in Colorado in the early 1980's made us a somewhat displaced family. My husband was determined to start our path as pioneers of the West. It was just us. We did not have a foe or friend in this place. No relatives to connect to. We visited Colorado the year before we moved. We were determined when we left the Red Rock's concert that Colorado was the place we would settle. No Job prospects, no place to stay, we moved with a six-week-old baby in tow. We traveled from the South to Ohio to visit my husband's family before heading to Colorado. My mother-in-law suggested that I stay in Ohio with her while my husband traveled ahead to set things up. My husband was determined. We were going together. I thought his mom's idea was a good one. I was happy to stay in the comfort of her home instead of venturing into the unknown.

Our phone bills were outrageous the first few years, because of the frequent calls to home. I was scared.

I met some wonderful people in Colorado, but I was anxious to have true friends. We met Gaile and Chuck Howard. They were "displaced" from Alabama and the East Coast. I met others through them. They were the ones who would introduce us to Pauline and her family. Years later, Gaile and Chuck moved back home. They were the only people that felt like family in an ocean of lonely wilderness. I felt sad but glad for them. They were moving closer to their family. I envied that.

But God blessed us with other friends that felt like family. I was grateful for starting to feel at home again in Colorado. I did not feel at home first. As we made more friends, those connections started to make me feel safe. But it was not until I met and got to know

Pauline that I started to feel secure in our new home. She most certainly was not a southern girl. We initially became friends because we both had qualities that each other admired. We did not realize those were the things in us that we needed to develop and appreciate in ourselves. My smart self-awakened when I met Pauline. She was always able to push and encourage me to be the person that I am. It was almost as if she could recognize the things in me that kept me from achieving my highest goals. I would often ask for her to proofread or review of my school papers or work reports. Whether they were from my seminary courses or my writing of book reviews. She was a true teacher in the friendship realm. She encouraged me to operate in excellence.

Pauline supported the ideas and projects I wanted to manifest. She was often the mirror I needed to reflect on when I was in my creative process. Pauline also supported me when I decided to go back to school for my master's degree. She believed in me. There were moments I lost my academic confidence along the way. Pauline kept me focused and motivated during those times.

Fortunately, I made good grades while I was in school. Having good grades open doors for me to prove my abilities on a larger scale. Working with Pauline also helped me appreciate my own academic abilities. I worked with her on various community projects. I saw that I had what it took to pursue some of my own dreams too.

Pauline and I cultivated a good and solid friendship. We didn't always see eye to eye. We had mutual friends tell us that we were just alike in our approach. We have been called twins on several occasions.

We nurtured and watched our kids grow up together. We went on family adventures. We rooted each other on. We had a lot in common when it came to sharing our talents, hopes and dreams. With another astounding woman, we joined a planning committee for community engagement. We became the founders of a relevant and viable non-profit community organization. It was God's plan for us to combine our talents for God's glory.

And for that experience, I will be forever grateful. I am able to spread my wings in my vocation and purpose in life. I am confident and assured that we have and will have a positive impact on the lives of others. Pauline taught me how to move my ideas to the next level. Especially when the intention supports the greater good. Pauline is a dedicated community leader and has a passion for the health and wellbeing of others Just like me. I am grateful for her shedding light on my capabilities to accomplish my goals. We have been through a lot together. And yes, we cried together....

Can we see eye to eye?
Twins in mind and soul
Friends in heart and in God
*Blessed to be the ties that bind…..**thelma craig***

Chapter 25
Tee Tee-Dream Angel

I had a dream the night before she came back from her trip to Hawaii. I could not wait to share the dream with her. I burst into her office and closed the door. She was just as excited as I was.

She said, "I have something for you."

She wanted me to share my dream with her. But she also had something to share with me. We fought for the chance to go first. She relented and I told her about my dream.

I had dreamed that I was dressed in the most colorful and vibrant fabric. My head was wrapped in a colorful headdress. I was flying in the dream. I was flying through the sky like a bird. I was moving in circles around a vast sky. I was feeling elated and in awe as I flew about in my rem sleep state. When I woke up, I felt my dream meant something powerful. Because years earlier, I'd gone home during school break during college. I was sitting by the pot belly wood stove and my grandmama was poking the fire. She stared at me and said, "Sister, I saw you flying."

I asked her, "What does that mean, grandmama?"

She looked at me with her strait-laced expression and said, "You are not ready yet child to hear the truth." I kept that memory in my heart and my mind forever. She would not tell me what that meant at the time. She died before we got to talk about it again.

So, when I woke from the dream many years later, I knew it was connected.

I couldn't wait to share my dream with TT. She always delighted in hearing about my dreams. I liked the stories she shared as well. After I told her about my dream it was time for her to share her exciting news. She had to sit up and take a deep breath. Her faced was flushed as she slowly told me what she had for me. She told me about how she was just taking a walk in Maui in the shops. She was attracted by this little gift shop because she had just spotted an item with the most vibrant colors in the window. It was a miniature, cocoa brown ornament that was hanging from the ceiling. Like it was flying. It was a small statue of a Black woman dressed in a beautiful headwrap and a multicolored dress. The arms of this miniature woman were sprawled out holding feathers in both hands. It moved about the room when the door opened as though it was flying. TT unwrapped the gift and presented it to me. We both stood there in awe. That was me in my dream. That little lady continues to fly high in my home foyer. You can always see her flying and thriving.

Her name was just as unique as she was to my life. We called her T2. Her first name, maiden name and her married name all began with T's. When I met her I immediately felt the Spirit of my Great Grandmama. She was White, quick-witted, feisty, humorous, wise and warm. She was from the hippie and civil rights era. She had strong feminist opinions and spoke her mind on controversial subjects at the drop of a hat. She was a force to be reckoned with.

This new manager of the department I worked in was a God send. She came to me in my life at a time I needed a breakthrough at work. Ya'll know how it is. Being a strong Black woman in the workplace, I was often misunderstood.

You know the battles we fought—the ones that depicted us as angry women. No matter how we genuinely appeared, we were often labeled as troublemakers on the job. We just wanted to be treated fairly and with respect. That's another book...
I loved my Job and the work we did. I liked the fact that I was supporting and helping the community. TT came with that same passion and intention. She was the type of woman who would've been on the Underground Railroad helping our people find their freedom. She had a Spirit with a mission. She was the gift that we needed as a people to open doors that were difficult to open. She was a modern-day abolitionist. She was also approaching a time in her life where she was ready to retire.

TT had a heart of gold. And she used it in that department before she departed. She supported and opened so many doors for others in dead-end jobs due to discrimination and workplace injustice.

TT was interested in the empowerment and equity of all people before equity became the buzz word. But somehow this woman saw and understood my plight and my pain. After she arrived at the department, she immediately invited staff to come to her and tell them about themselves and their roles. I was a little hesitant at first but I felt she was sincere. I went and shared the issues and challenges I had experienced in our work environment. She listened intently and was so in tuned and open, that I shared some more. I presented myself as who I was. I told her how I loved my Job but was stifled and hindered due to a political and often racially oppressive climate.

I had worked there for almost fifteen years and felt that I was not valued nor had I received well overdue promotions. I let my guard down talking to her. She understood. We connected on so many levels. We would drive to Grand Junction for meetings. As we traveled through those beautiful mountains, we listened to music by Shirley Horn, Etta James and Aretha Franklin. We laughed, cried and shared our hearts.

TT asked me to write my new Job description and my ideas about how to promote the programs my department facilitated. She also requested a proposal on how I could support the department in meeting program objectives in serving the community in HIV/AIDS Care and Treatment. I did as I was told. I was soon promoted and working in a new position. It was a huge blessing. I was able to spread my wings and provide service to our communities in a way I knew would really make a difference. She gave me the opportunity to feel good about the work I was doing. She allowed me the space, platform and freedom to enhance my occupation and my calling. I saw how we are sometimes placed in positions and jobs that allow us to fulfill our purpose on a larger scale to glorify God.

I could see the by and by. I was grateful for my new assignment and work and for TT. She was a light that will always shine in me. God place people or Angels in or lives to open doors, to make the path easy. They bless you with opportunity and Joy.

Spread your wings,
Fly high and mighty, Soar
You are the daughter they left to do the work
*Serve justice to higher heigh*ts...***thelma craig***

Chapter 26
Lynette - Sister Strength

My second semester in college was confusing for me. I decided to leave and not return after the first semester break. I had actually given up until my Mama persuaded me not to.

"Go on back, baby. Everything is going to be alright."

Mama had received a letter from my roommate telling her that she suspected I would not return the second semester. The nerve of her writing my mama! That was a very bold friend and I will tell you all about her the next chapter.

It was like I had known Lynette all my life. She was a saucy Southern girl that came with tremendous hospitality. She was so sweet. In our Social Psychology class, I had the pleasure of speaking during the class discussion only to be matched by this cute little lady who reminded me of me. We agreed on the issue of the discussion. She smiled at me in a show of support for my statements. I smiled back assuring her that we connected on an intellectual level. I acknowledged the spiritual connection as well. I knew that I had found a kindred Spirit.

We acknowledged each other while filing out of class with mutual smiles. Lynette was a short, cute, coco-colored, bright-eyed young lady. Her Southern charm and grace were ever present. She called you by those sweet, warm colloquialisms that I heard my grandmas use. Names like suky, sugar, honey babe.

She softly touched you when she was communicating in a reassuring way.

She had a confidence which I know now was her faith. She had a faith beyond measure at that age. And I saw myself in her. I would soon understand the meaning of another lesson of how to walk by faith and not by sight.

Lynette came into my life for a good reason. The following week after that dynamic class discussion, I answered a knock on my dorm door. It was Lynette! I wondered how she knew where my dorm was located. Her visit was a pleasant surprise.

She was a bit rushed when she asked, "Do you have a black slip I can borrow?" My eyes widened. I thought it must be a coincidence. I was just home during school break and my mother admonished me for not having a slip to wear underneath a somewhat skimpy dress I'd put on to wear to church. She had just purchased a black slip for me.

"I quickly said, "Yes, Lynette. I have one. I opened my dresser drawer and retrieved the black slip my mama just bought and handed it to Lynette.

"Let me get a bag for you to carry it in ".

"No need."

She saw the surprise in my face and hurriedly explained to me why she needed it.

Lynette lived off campus in the Atlanta metro area. She was fortunate to have a car to commute to school. I learned and marveled about her large family and her six loving sisters that lived close by. Lynette lived with one of them. She did not have the time to drive all the way from campus to her house to get a slip. Her boyfriend was pledging a fraternity and she had just been invited to be his escort to an impromptu event. Lynette explained how she often saw me go towards this dorm after class. She said she kept a mental note because she wanted to introduce herself to me and get acquainted. She realized that she needed a slip because the dress she had in her car was sheer. She said I was the first person that came to her mind when she thought about who she felt comfortable enough to borrow underwear from. We both laughed at that. I too could not think of another person besides her I would borrow underwear from.

Its uncanny how you just trust a person immediately. I felt that faith in her from the start. We graduated from college together and remained friends after college. I would spend weekends at her sister's home and they always treated me like one of them. She was a great model of southern hospitality. She always cooked me a home cooked meal. I slept on the most comfortable, fresh beds and linen. What a great treat from my college dorm amenities.

Lynette was the youngest of her sisters. They adored her and she them. She was the youngest but seemed like the oldest. She was always talking about her sisters, brothers, Mom and Daddy. They were her purpose during those times. I admired her strong family values. I appreciated that she loved her siblings.

Lynette had six of the most loving and caring people in her life. They were just as loving and supporting of the people she introduced them to. She brought me into her circle of sisters. I didn't meet all of them. But somehow, I knew they knew me. When I met one of her sisters she beamed. She seemed to love me because she felt Lynette loved me. She welcomed me into their family.

Lynette got her strength from her family. She thought highly of her mother. She told me that her mother was a pillar of strength and faith. That was where she inherited it from.

I hoped that me and my sisters—both biological and community sisters—would encourage each other like that. That is the natural way. To use our faith to encourage each other. What better message of courage to get from a woman of faith. Always providing words of encouragement and hopefulness. I could always share my fears and concerns with Lynette and receive the best advice of remaining faithful. Where I saw no way, she always saw a way. She always had scripture and words of wisdom to console or advise me with. When I listened to her, I left feeling that things would be alright. Her faith in God was omnipresent. Over the years, I watched Lynette go through the loss of her parents with grace. She went through her grief with the assistance of the Spirit of faith. She always had a profound word about how God was working in her life and would see her through.

She was that way about every obstacle that came on her path. She always said that God would make a way out of no way.

Lynette was one of seven bridesmaids at my wedding. I was still residing in Atlanta but planning my wedding in Florida. We were just out of college and did not have very much financial income. Lynette promised she could afford the wedding expenses (i.e. bridesmaid gown and shoes). She also assured me that she could make the travel expense to Florida. When she missed her first travel arrangements, I began to worry. She called the morning of the wedding from the bus station. I was oh so happy. She traveled and trudged many hours on that bus to be there for me. My mama picked her up and immediately liked her. She said you have found a friend for life.

Over the years, we have remained friends. I witnessed from afar and at close range how her faith in God strengthens every year. We sometimes do not see each other for years but we always keep in touch by phone. Oftentimes the conversation is about our faith in God. It was as if we never had the time and distance between our talks. We just picked up from where we last talked.

Lynette and her husband dreamed of having a baby. They'd had a few challenges in getting pregnant but I would always hear how much faith she had in God to the day she gave birth to her healthy baby boy. I was blessed to be there when she finally delivered a beautiful healthy son. I always admired her confidence and faithfulness when she became a mother.

We have shared our joys and many experiences of life over the years. Lynette's faith strengthens my faith. She used her faith to help her heal from cancer.

That challenge and the subsequent victory made her faith even stronger. Never did I ever think Lynette would face such a test. Yet she continues in her faith journey. Today, she is cancer free!

I'm sure Lynette gets weary sometimes. But I have never heard a weary word. I am so proud of her and her unwavering trust in God.

I heard her quote the scripture, "With God, all things are possible." And I am blessed to know that kind of woman. It allows me to see the work of God up close. It helps me to remain faithful. I understand why she is in my life and I am truly grateful. As I witness her faith, it strengthens mine.

Walk in stride
Talk with hope, with gentle assurance
Eyes and heart open wide
*Encouraging us with leaps of faith….***thelma craig**

Chapter 27
Donna – My Roomie

I was leaving home for the first time to go to a school in what you would call *the big city*. I was a country girl. A sheltered, innocent baby just leaving home for the first time. I am a real country girl with all the naiveté of the world.

I met my very first roommate who was already moved into the dorm when I arrived to the campus. She was a beautiful, caramel-colored woman with stark, almost handsome appearance. She walked in that tough city girl power. She was from a big city on the east coast. She was ready for life and she was ready for me.

She checked me on my outfit without hesitation. We were getting dressed for freshman orientation. With exasperation, laughter and a little bit of force she said, "Why you country bumpkin you, if you don't get in there and take off that damn lime green dress! You are not going in that damn auditorium and embarrass yourself or me."

She laughed while I went back to change into some jeans as that what she was wearing. I was shocked that she laughed at and disliked my dress. The dress was that year's Easter dress. It was lime green polyester with a sheer flora laced shoulder covering.

That was the beginning of Donna teaching me how to show up as my best, with confidence, in my own style with the grace that already existed in me.

I was just a little country girl who hadn't gotten use to the big city life. I did not know I needed to be more assertive than before.

Donna was assertive, aggressive and confident. I showed up docile, reserved and reluctant. Hell, I was scared. Where she was hard in her approach, I was soft. We complimented each other in that way. Where she often approached a difficult situation with harshness, I approached it with sensitivity.

I recognized that the confident and assertiveness energy was in me too. And Donna could approach things gently when she wanted to. It seemed that our opposite attributes had laid dormant in us until we saw them in each other.

She was always talking about how you must show up. It wasn't that I didn't have style in my dress or appearance. I had just moved away from home, my safe place. I knew that you had to dress the part wherever you were, on every occasion. My mama taught me that as well. I was just a bud not yet in full bloom. It was my time to begin the blooming process.

Donna shed light on that which was already in me. By the grace of God, I learned how to go to a thrift store in an affluent neighborhood and find just the right outfit with meager funds. As Donna would say, we were struggling college students and we had to find the best way to survive and still look outstanding. This girl had the confidence and boldness of a rock and the assurance of a bolt of lightning. She knew how to walk into a concert without blinking an eye. She coached me on how to do it at the Fox theatre one time. She said, all you have to do is look the part. Wear the right clothes, shoes that make you walk boldly into the door.

"You got to look like you are the performer and the star and are about to get up on that stage."

"Hold your head up, point your toes in a direction, flash your ID and walk on through the door without showing a blink of fear to the ticket taker." We always got in free.

She coached me on several occasions on how to take a more assertive stand. And I showed her how to take it down a notch. We fought that first year. We were trying to get to know each other. We kept running into ourselves and often we didn't like what we saw. But the lessons persisted. We walked to the back entrance to the Democratic National Convention, past the first security and entered when the U.S. Representative Andrew Young and his entourage showed up.

Donna stepped up to security staff and said, "Hi. my name is Donna Wilson. We are with the US Representative." The Officer looked at us, smiled, nodded his head and said, "Come on, young ladies. Happy you are here."

My mouth flew open, then I remembered Donna telling me not to show too much reaction. Keep the serious look. We walked the red carpet to the front of the grounds. We fared well the rest of the evening. We attended the after parties, blended in all the crowds and were treated like we were special invited guests. We would take a lot more adventures. I got my dare on, my boldness emerged. I always thought that was amazing. I hope I was just as impactful. I hope I gave her a calm and a reflection of softness that was my gift to her.

By the end of the first semester, I was ready to quit school. I left for home on Christmas break certain I would not return. I was exhausted from trying to grow. Learning in5 the college classroom is just as intriguing as learning life lessons of growing up and navigating relationships.

I was assured of that when my mama told me she received a letter from my roommate. The letter outlined the challenges and experiences I had in my first semester. Donna was bold enough to share with my mother how she saw me work out God's Plan. She told my mama that despite our differences, she believed we were friends and that we were meant to meet. She said she'd learned a lot from me and was certain I learned a lot from her. She encouraged my mother to convince me to return to school next semester.

My mother laughed and said, "She was bold. But she was right." My mother agreed that I should not give up because I had the same qualities in me and just needed to put them to work. I had to go back and face Donna and myself. My mother told me to continue to learn from friends but to let God set the pace for my life. Mama said God sent certain people to help you bring out things in you that you need to survive in this world. Confidence, power and bringing out my voice was what

Donna came to teach me. I came to teach her softness and compassion for those around her. This was another beginning and a rebirth to becoming a woman. The mirror of God was doing its work.

We had quite a journey navigating our first year of college and moving through the complexities of friendship. We were both trying to find our way. It was time again for me to see my power and strength at a most vulnerable period of my life. My first college roommate taught me to breathe it all in. She shared her strengths and weaknesses with me. I offered the same without knowing that's why we were put on the path together.

She prompted me to look at myself, to turn myself forward and embrace my character, my looks and my power. I am not giving her all the credit. This is who I was being prepared to be through all the women that came before her and the women whose lessons were yet to come. I am certain my parents were trying to teach me some of these same lessons. But when I got to college, I was bound to start looking at myself through my core. I was primed for the awareness to embrace who I was and use all my gifts to propel me forward. I understand in this by and by.

The tides coming fast and furious
The rain beating hard on the ground
The wind and the test of time blows
All great qualities to have in self,
Bringing out the beauty of nature as who we are each
*season....**thelma craig***

Chapter 28
Ma – Mother-in-Love

When I first met her, she smiled the most wonderful smile I have ever seen. It was sweet and absorbing. I met her before I met her son. Interestingly, I met his father, mother and other siblings before I met him. My mother-in-law was a lovely anomaly. At first, I bought into the myth and lies that Mother-in-laws are supposed to be mean, malicious and unkind. Not this one. That's why we should be mindful not to pre-judge women based on what others have experienced. Especially when we concede that God has placed special women in our lives to teach and nurture us.

It is imperative that we embrace the blessed women God presents to us. The good and the not so good experiences with others come to teach us. The healing part of acknowledging the women in my life. I had my own unique experience with Ma Craig. During my time getting to know and knowing her, I asked myself many times, "Where did I get such negative assumptions about mother-in-law?" Undoubtedly, it was television and the movies because I had never been married before. We often make assumptions about people before getting to know them. I learned from Ma Craig, the joy of getting to know a mother other than your biological Mother. Some of us have multiple women in our lives that fit the second mother position.

When I first met her, I thought she was a bit annoyed with me because my husband's father, her husband, took an immediate liking to me. He laughed at everything I said. He got excited when I entered the room. He didn't spare attention and devotion to me when they visited us in Atlanta. He was a charming man that adored her dearly. He was a funny, gentle man. I watched him with her, he called her" dear". I knew where her son got his gentleman spirit from. My husband calls me "dear".

During that visit, Ma Craig's husband, future (father in Law) could not stop talking about me. He listened to my every word after asking my opinion about an uncertain issue or topic. In several instances, Ma Craig had to tell him to stop pestering me. Of course, he was playful and ignored her harmless admonishment. I began to think she blamed me for his attention. I realized later that she liked me too. Later, after I married her son, our respect and admiration for each other grew deeply. I really liked how she loved and admired her nine children. I witnessed and heard her express that love all the time. She also loved and admired her husband. And she observed how my husband and I interacted. One bit of wisdom she gave us we still follow to this day. She told us to kiss and hug each other every time we leave the house and when we return. No matter how mad we were at each other.

After her son and I got married she began to visit us often. She was there for the birth of our children. She was there to truly lend a hand. She loved her grandchildren even more. I used to wonder lovingly, *how could a woman have so much love and patience for so many children?* My husband confirmed that she *was* loving but she was also stern. She was the disciplinarian being that she had to discipline mostly sons. He shared the time she broke up boy sibling fight with a broom handle. I have seen that side of her during my time knowing her.

Our mutual respect was what I cherished most about this woman. During her visits, she and I would sit at the kitchen table and share the most intimate conversations. She was a southern belle from Alabama. Her mother moved her from Alabama when she was very young. She was a great cook. The best. My mama taught me how to cook but I learned to appreciate the way other mamas cooked. She taught me how to make peach cobbler, sweet potato pie and the famous Craig Christmas cookies. Now my daughter has the recipe and makes them every year. I spent lots of phone bill money calling her to ask instructions about a certain recipe. Ma Craig was my phone chef. We used to annoy my husband when we were in the kitchen together.

Not wanting to hurt or offend each other we always said, "I make it like this but you go ahead and make it like that. You make it the way you want. I'll just love the way you do it.

"You do it the best way. You go on and make it your way."

We went back and forth like this until I conceded. She was the queen in the kitchen. Her way to prepare the dish was the best way. I asked her questions and she gladly and thoughtfully answered.

I was working at the State Health Department in the Disease Control section. I worked as a Disease Control Specialist helping to prevent the spread of sexually transmitted diseases. Ma Craig would get really engrossed in learning about the work I did. She wanted to know how diseases were transmitted. She wasn't naive, she just hadn't heard some of the things I shared with her about sex.

Ma Craig was from the old school and was not privy to the intriguing new things people were doing in the sex arena. This was when the Syphilis epidemic and the HIV/AIDS outbreak took place.

I was learning from her and she was learning from me. She asked me questions because she believed women didn't know everything, they should know to protect themselves.

Ma Craig always came to support us while we were raising the kids. I think she just wanted to hear the latest news about what was happening. She listened intently without judgment. I will always cherish her visits and our talks. My daughter went to stay with her when she was just three years old. To this day, I swear my daughter reminds me of her grandmother. She even looks and acts like her with her slow and deliberate way of moving about. Thinking pensively about what somebody isn't saying and having the patience of a saint.

The last time we saw her was at the nursing home. We surprised her with a visit. She was looking good and exhibited soundness of thought and mind. My husband greeted her first. As she sat enjoying her son's company, she turned to the sound of somebody approaching her from behind.

"I know that walk. I feel that Thelma is approaching. I can feel her presence."

She knew me and I knew her. My husband knows us both. He always says how I act like his mother. She has truly blessed us both. I understand that Ma Craig was a gift to me.

Wade in the water
Walk on the sand
Show me how to be the woman,
*by holding my hand…..**thelma craig***

Chapter 29
Miss Willie Mae- Step to it Mama

My Daddy always said he would never marry again. He and my mother separated when I was nine years old and I think the divorce was final after seventeen years. I was shocked when Daddy called to tell me that he was getting married. He was 68 and she was 58. We were attending an annual family gathering when he introduced me to this saucy, long-legged, classy yet, hip, elegant Black woman. I was in awe of her. I didn't know what to think. The first person that came to mind was my Great Grandmother. She reminded me of her with her stature and aura. I would say that she was sassy and the "sapphire women that my dad liked. This woman was taller than my daddy, well dressed and what my Daddy would call, rough cut and stern. A sapphire. He lovingly called Black women. She reminded me of a couple of my grandmothers and all the other women rolled into one. She was obviously beautiful to my Daddy. I had to accept that he made his choice and I would respect it.

A few days before the wedding, Miss Willie Mae called me to say, "I hope you know that when yo Daddy and I get married, I'm the one in charge. I know how much your Daddy love his children, but I'm here to tell you and you need to know that If something happens to him, I'm the one that will inherit all of it." I thought, *Its not like my daddy had millions.*

I just swallowed and said, "Okay."

I didn't share what she said with my Daddy until years after she died.

I learned how to be gracious and just let things go. My Daddy was no fool. He knew what he was getting into. My Daddy was a meticulous and cantankerous old man by that time. I was not in control of my Daddy's life, but I was his baby girl and I watched over him. While Miss Willie and I watched each other, I had to trust that he knew what he was getting into.

I guess our parents said the same about us when we made decisions that are likely to change our lives significantly. I just breathed. Daddy had his reason for marrying her and I'm sure he had his best interest at heart. She always tried to put her best foot forward with him. Especially when it came to his kids.

She knew that he had a love for his children that would make him question others if they cast them in a bad light. My father was the kind of Daddy that would say, "I can talk about my kids, but you can't." So, I never shared with him the conversation she had with me. It wasn't until his last year on the planet that I shared with him some of the things she had said to me. I just let it be.

Before his death, while he was sitting with me waiting to die, I was blessed to witness his atonement process. I was able to experience his reflection on how he performed during his life. He admitted that he had regrets. He also said there were mistakes he made that he couldn't do nothing about. To his credit, I witnessed him making an attempt to correct those mistakes.

He shared with me his personal insights on the loves of his life. What each woman meant to him. Because of Miss Willie Mae, I was able to show my Daddy that I trusted him. It was his life and he was a grown man. I was mature enough to know that he was his own man. During the last few years I was blessed with the opportunity to ask my Daddy questions that I would never think I would ask a man from the old school. Miss Willie Mae left an impression on us all.

Daddy explained that Miss Willie Mae bought something new and refreshing to his life. They started traveling and exploring new places. He appeared to be happy. She also introduced him to the age of computers. She enrolled him in computer classes. She escorted him to concerts and classic nightlife activities for older people. She encouraged him to attend and join the church. Her influence was so great, that he became a member of the usher board. Daddy always believed in God; he was just not a churchgoer in the beginning. Miss Willie Mae had that kind of influence. She encouraged him to study the bible with her. I saw my Daddy pray along with her. He told me about the ritual they had in the morning before they made up the bed together. He said they would get on their knees and pray together. Miss Willie Mae shared her spiritual self with my Daddy, and for the most part, I always heard her speak highly of God. For this I am grateful for Miss Willie Mae.

My Daddy was a lover of women. He told me so. That was his weakness so to say. He loved his kids and the women in his life. The kids were the priority. He told me that every woman he ever loved in his life was important and special to him in their own way. He loved and cherished my mom, his first wife, even though they just couldn't get along. Miss Willie Mae seemed to bring a certain Joy to his life. She had her quirks, but it was not my job to judge. He loved her so I had to like her. I will leave that right there. Because I think I saw some qualities in her that are in me. She was fine and stern.

After he and my mother separated, I often heard my father say that he would never marry again. Their marriage failing had not only hurt him but other people he loved and cared for. To watch his hopes and dreams melt away—dreams of being settled in a community, raising kids—was really hard for him. He surprised me when he married again late in his life. He seemed to be content as a bachelor.

He'd met a woman that he believed he would grow older with. One he could take care of and her taking care of him. Even though she was ten years younger than he was at the time. Miss Willie Mae was a presence. She was different. She took my Daddy by storm. He was happy and warmed up to the idea of being married again. He had his motives, I'm sure of it. They enjoyed the new activities. He enjoyed traveling with her. He jumped into that phase of his life with new vigor and excitement. Miss Willie bought another level of Joy to his life.

Like I said, she was a hostess with the mostess. My Daddy had hospitality skills unmatched. This too was where they complimented each other. My Daddy was always the life of the party. Miss Willie Mae always used her fine china, linen and decorative accents. She made an ordinary visit spectacular. She showed me new ways to entertain and host with flair. She served with a theme in mind. I learned not to wait for tomorrow to enjoy the moment of serving your guests with your best china. And that's why Miss Willie Mae is one of the women that impacted my life. She had a style that I admired.

Miss Willie Mae brought some happy times to my Daddy's later years. Although he lived many years after her, I don't think he regretted making that change. She played the stepmother role when the Spirit led her. She was pleasantly stubborn. She was a gracious hostess when we came to visit. She cooked wonderful dinners along with my Daddy in the kitchen. She planned excursions in and around West Palm Beach that were fit for royalty. We took a cruise to the Bahamas one evening, gambled and turned back to the city port. I remember the time she and my Daddy took us to a Ray Charles Concert in Palm Beach at the *Kravis Center for Performing Arts.* It was spectacular and elegant event.

My husband and I had such a good time with my Daddy and his wife. A few days after we retuned home, Miss Willie Mae mailed me a package that included my blue panties I left in the guest bedroom under the bed sheets. She included a note that said, "I guess you had a good time". Her sense of humor matched my dad's. She was a catalyst for helping Daddy carry out his best assets. Hospitality, humor

195

and a relationship with God. She considered herself a staunch Christian Woman. She was a praying Woman. She was adamant about prayer and bible study time.

It was great experiencing my Daddy while I was an adult. Sitting in his and hers recliners, I was permitted to share with him all the things you don't think you could share with a parent. I shared with him how I felt growing up. I told him what my experiences were like when he and my mama divorced. He was able to share with me about some of his experiences as well. He told me about his relationship with Miss Willie Mae. He admitted he missed her. He experienced a great sense of loneliness when she died.

I began to see them as a team. She bought out the best in him and she received something from him in return. I'm sure some other not-so-flattering sides showed up in their relationship. But for the most part, I witnessed a happy man connecting to a great woman in his late years. They were OK together as far as I could see. OK. Who am I to judge?

If she had something to say, she would tell you point blank, behind Daddy's back of course. Daddy told me she got into a fight with her past husband and he shot her. Then she shot him back with the pistol she always carried in her car. I wonder if this is why I treaded lightly with Miss Willie Mae. She had no problem taking a person to the side to let you know just how she felt about things. I refused to speak ill of her. This was a powerful, strong, Black woman who endured a lot.

Then she chose to marry my Daddy as ornery as he was in his old age. I realized that she did deserve my respect and that's why I always gave it to her.

Even though we don't immediately embrace the sister-women that show up in our lives, they each come with their own powerful lessons and purpose. I gave it sometime and now I appreciate the gift of her. What God intended for her to teach me.

After Miss Willie Mae died and I was supporting my Daddy in planning her funeral, I realized the purpose and the lessons she imparted. She also taught me to remember what my Daddy always told me "You love em', I like em'." That person may not be who you want for your loved one, but you should respect their choice.

Many years later, as my Daddy was preparing for his pending death, we talked about his marriage to Miss Willie Mae. I understand by and by what she meant to him and how his love for her and her love for him had impacted my life.

Stature, stamina and powerful presence
A force to be reckoned with
Leaving you wondering and seeing
*The wind blows towards your growth…***thelma craig**

Chapter 30
Nikki-Sister in Love

At one of my wedding showers the guests were asked to write a message to me about me getting married and what I would carry with me for the rest of my life. The stationery was laced with iris and had a smooth circular edge. I finally settled down and realized I was *married now*. I sat in a quiet spot to open the wedding memory booklet and read the messages. I read some sweet, thoughtful, heartfelt, funny messages. Adorable passages or one-two sentences of hope and blessings for my new life. Some of them wrote about how they knew God would be with me and Jeff.

A couple of the notes spoke of how happy people were for me and prayed for nothing but happiness for me and my husband. It was such a sweet bridal shower. The idea and gesture was to shower me with love and grace. I was so not present for all the showers of love cast on me. I missed a lot. It wasn't until later that I began to cherish the moments. My Sister-in -Love wrote:

Dear God,
I love Jeffrey and Thelma so much. I thank you so much for them. I pray dear God for a life filled with the love and eternal Joy as they begin their lives together. May they always find answers to problems through prayers. Bless them, stay close and may they always remember you care and love

them. Much happiness to them always. Thank you – Amen, Nikki.

I didn't cry until years later while reading these gems of messages in my wedding memory book. Throughout the years of our marriage, Nikki has always showed me that Sister Love. She always has positive and endearing things to say to me. She always treated me like I was a part of her family.

Nikki was often the peacemaker in our family. I was always assured that when people come to her with a message about somebody else in the family, she never spoke badly of them. She always tried to see the good in the person.

There were many occasions when I felt I was being attacked by someone in the family. My husband shared it with his sister Nikki. She always took a deep breath and sat quiet. She always avoided and averted negativity. My husband is most like her in character.

I read a prayer on social media that made me think of Nikki. It said, "Always pray to have eyes that see the best in people, a heart that forgives the worst, and a mind that forgets the bad and a soul that never loses faith in God."

Those are powerful instructions to live by. I don't think I have mastered those things, but I see them in Nikki.

Hold up the banner of Love
Move through a garden of loving-kindness
Tap to the beat of my heart
*God is blessing us…..**thelma craig***

Chapter 31
Just a Bit of a Jewel

I have this song in my head sometimes from a childhood memory by Sonny Charles & The Checkmates, Ltd. 1969
Black pearl, precious little girl
Let me put you up where you belong
Black pearl, little girl,
You've been in the background for much too long
 You been working so hard your whole life through…
        She's all that and more. A special woman. A most admired woman to many. She was never in the background in my heart.

        This close relative, I admired for as far back as I can remember. I was a little impressionable girl when I first saw her. She was always a part of my life because she was older than me, of course. I so wanted to be as beautiful as she was because I was told by my peers that I wasn't. But when she came around, I knew I had a chance.

        I always thought I looked like her. At least I wanted to look like her. She was dark, elegant, smart and the life of the party. When she came to family gatherings, my heart latched onto her. She was what they called *fine*. She wore the coco dark skin I inherited like it was the greatest gesture in the world. She had a nice body with a big round shapely butt. I don't have the shapely legs she has; I got my legs from my mother (they called mama's legs chicken legs). But that didn't keep me from imagining I had beautiful legs like this relative. She was always stylish with impeccable taste in clothes and accessories. When I saw her as a child, my little heart jumped and said, that's me when I get older. I loved myself some her. She could do no wrong in my eyes. She seemed to know how to do everything. She brought with her the high fashion from the north. She hosted parties, family reunions and fashion shows with flare. She visited with style. When she came to town, everyone took notice. She was one of the family members that migrated to the North. The South and its Jim Crow antics made a lot of my uncles, cousins and aunts to migrate to the North. When she came back home to visit, I thought the North was heaven, because she resided there. She was so amazing and intoxicating to my little mind. She looked at me as if she knew that I admired her.

I loved the way she loved her daughters. She was a great mother. We cultivated the relationship well into my adulthood. My Daddy loved and took care of her. She was an apple in his eye. He was glad that I loved and admired her too. Somewhere I got lost in my admiration for her. I tried to emulate her style of dress. My soul wanted her to admire me too. I thought I was her favorite relative. I put her on a pedestal in my heart and mind. What I learned is, you shower your most high praise only on God. Needless to say, I was young and innocent. And I was heartbroken for MY mistaken devotion to a person. I will always and still hold her in high esteem. I realize you can be devoted to persons in your life, but it should be from a place of balance and understanding of their humanness. Keep your esteem for yourself.

God is your ultimate source. The scripture teaches us, *"I will seek ye first the kingdom of God and all other things and people will come to me".* When it came to this Jewel, my discernment was a bit off. People have flaws but I didn't see any in her. I thought she set the moon. I still do.

I continue to believe my Jewel is a great person, I love and admire her. At the time of this writing, we had not spoken in a while. I write about this jewel, only to say, people come into our life for a reason and a season. So, understand the significance of relationships and what they bring to us; and how they influence us.   We must value these blessings yet find balance in them all. She is valuable in my heart. Like my mama always said, we will understand better by and by.

Reflection in my stare,
Beauty in my Pearlie eyes
Behold the shine of us
Soul and heart with irregular beats
See the jewel in the oyster shell…..thelma craig

Chapter 32
Levonne – Prayer Warrior

Have you ever met a woman and immediately know that she is a powerful woman of God? Because of her smile, I immediately saw the light in Levonne. She was a new woman at the Health Department where I worked. There were so few Blacks working there, I always made it my business to meet them, introduce myself when they arrive. I walked over to the building and section where I heard we had a new African American employee. And she was a Sister! I walked over to the adjacent building into her office and was immediately lit up by her smile. I tell you it was her smile and her faith in God that help me make it through some tough moments on the job. She is a bit younger than I am, yet she had an old Spirit. We all know the struggles and the challenges we have on the job in this racist environment. I am here to tell you that had my challenges. She was a work "prayer warrior". We need them in our work life.

When I first moved to Colorado, I had to file a discrimination lawsuit at one of my previous Jobs. It was an experience with blatant discrimination and toxicity. I fought like hell and won. This coworker actually told me that she could not understand why I am working there in a high-level position and not in the janitorial department. After so many insults and unfair treatment in that department, I had no other choice but to file a lawsuit against management. Long story, after filing with EEOC, this department was required to coordinate what they called back then, "Sensitivity trainings". On the day the memo came to it announce that our little work group had to attend this first training session, the women in question was so upset and offended, she stood in front of me and slapped the can drink I had in my hand to the floor. To say the least, I was shocked. But by the grace of God I did not hit back. I ran out of the office and filed an assault and battery charge against her. But we learn to deal in these dysfunctional work environments. I did get stronger and a better work environment. Yet continued to have challenges. They were few and far between. They "departments" endeavored to have what they call now "Cultural Competency trainings".

Meeting Levonne enhanced my life in the workplace. Sure, I had already developed a thick skin when situations arrived with co- workers. However, I was still vulnerable, as time went on. I kept up my visits (to her office) with Levonne to get to know her. She was not one to come meet you until she got to know you. To this day, I still admire her discerning Spirit. It would prove to be necessary when I sought her advice with all things related to the work environment. She has a wisdom that is beyond her years. We soon became friends outside of work. She brings that prayer practice in everything -4we do.

One day, I was really struggling with a situation with a co- worker. I went to her office. No, I ran. She was there willing, ready to console, and to provide calming advice. Most importantly she always ready to pray with me. Right then and there, she took my hand, bowed her head and recited a prayer that lifted me up. Her words and sincerity were profound. We all need to be reminded, even in our work environment that God is with us.

Lavonne is a woman that is not afraid to pray (on the spot) and acknowledge that God is with us even in the workplace. I like it when she says, "Let's pray". She is a testament and a light to the Grace that God places people in your life to in places. Not only is she prayerful, she is smart and savvy when dealing with workplace politics. She is currently a institutional and Community Leader.

We sometimes have lapse about who we are in Christ, when placed in unfavorable situations. It can feel like the lion's den. Word says, "Cast ALL your cares upon him, for he cares for you" (1 Peter 5:7). That means, ALL our cares. I learned to breathe and trust that God will take care of me in the midst of the disorder on the job. So, I know that a prayer partner is necessary. Keep God with us in Everything we do. I knew that, yet she was an all-embracing reminder that we should not take God for granted, anywhere we go. I learned to Before, during and after meetings; during lunch and break, I carried God with me. Just a reminder here for you. I had a successful career for many years in the Department, I understood in the by and by.

Pray in the morning, Pray at night
Pray in the noon time, all times are right
God sends us angels to prompt our hope
*God send us angels to lift us up.....**thelma craig***

Chapter 33
Francis – Motherland

I always had a dream to visit and explore Africa. As a child growing up you only heard the Tarzan stories about the monkeys and the wild men in the jungle. I knew there was more to the story. I knew we had come from African Kings and Queens.

I would soon encounter the richness of African culture. I began to read books like the *Destruction of the African Civilization* by historian and literary icon, Dr. Chancellor Williams. I have to admit, I experienced anger and outrage when I read the story of the Middle Passage. I had read many books about the origin of our African culture. Learning the full truth about what happened to our ancestors made me feel indignant and radical. I began to proudly wear African garments, head dresses and colors that represented the Black struggle after my first year in college.

I began to decipher untruths I had been told about African people. I received a scholarship to go to Ghana. I was diverted. I later had the opportunity to go to South Africa. My dream had come to fruition through a Social Justice tour.

Once I arrived in South Africa, my anxiousness and eating different food caused me to become seriously constipated. I was unable to move my bowels for five of the eight days I was there. But the blessing of visiting the Motherland was still so great.

It taught me the importance of experiencing the joy in the moment and being in it gratefully. Not waiting for the by and by to revel in the grace of God.

In Atlanta, while I was in college, I met all kinds of people, from many places and stations. One of the people I met there was an African-born woman named Francis From Sierra Leon. She reminded me of the power, beauty and richness of my African roots.

During my experiences in Atlanta, I was still processing the feelings about awakening to the history of my ancestors, I felt free. I felt free from the taunts of childhood when bullies used to call me Black and ugly. I was attending a historically Black University and was ready to fully embrace and celebrate my blackness. I really grew up in Atlanta. It was a special passage from the dredges of the racist Florida. I did not know just how much until I went to a more progressive place. They still had challenges. But I was witness to the differences among my people and others. But I still lived in a pool of racism.

It was also in college in Atlanta that I discovered things had not totally changed. I was deeply dismayed and saddened when while walking down the street near campus, a Black man yelled out of his car at me, "Hey Blackie!" Fortunately, that experience was countered by a man who got out of his car and wanted to paint me and immortalize my beauty on canvas.

Shortly after that I met Francis. She was a Queen from Sierra Leon. She was the epitome of elegance, beauty, power and grace. She had a dark chocolate complexion with a powerful and attractive stature. She stood tall and acted tall. Her style of dress was impeccable. I also met her Sister Nina.

These women made me smile. I was so proud of their existence. All those myths and lies about Blackness not being beautiful were being dissolved.

Francis and Nina were friends of the brother of the man that would one day be my husband. They invited me to the African parties and gatherings. Francis and Nina shared with me that there was much turmoil in their country. Their family had come to America for refuge.

Francis and Nina had been born to a royal family. I learned so much about the problems Africa faced as a result of Westernism.

Francis and I bonded over delicious, traditional African food, hospitality and the warmth of their native culture. Francis and I forged a great friendship. She was a bridesmaid in my wedding and was on hand to welcome my first child. I watched and observed how she did things in her African culture. She always cooked and welcomed me into her home. She was adamant that you eat the food and got full. Cooking for me and others was Francis's way of showing that she really liked me. I caught on quickly.

I recall a time when Francis was working in a retail store selling music and albums. It was a very popular place to buy records at the time. In this store, you could encounter all kinds of people from perverts to regular old everyday music lovers. People loved to hang out at this music store to wait for the new releases or just freely listen to all kinds of music being played over the speaker system.

One day, while we were in the store, a young man approached Francis. He was rude and disrespectful. She looked him in the eye with a fierceness and told him if you don't go away, I will turn you into a pig. He went on his way. To this day, I still admire her power and strength in dealing with his disrespect.

Francis was a quiet storm. She was always sweet and kind, but she did not tolerate disrespect. I witnessed a quiet force in her that I will always admire. She was confident and secure. I loved that. She was the African queen that woke up the African queen inside of me.

The middle passage passed,
We cross winds and rain over the sea
Shackled in mind and body
Can't touch the Spirit in me....thelma craig

Chapter 34
I am ME

I am another woman that impacted my life. I take full responsibility for getting in my way sometimes. But I am human. I have my doubts and my fears. Ultimately, "I am as God created me."

I am very fond of that phrase from the <u>Course of Miracles</u> Workbook by Marianne Williamson. The book and workbook were given to me by one of my Spiritual Sisters, Leanne. When I first received the book, I didn't understand some of the materials. I realized many years after reading it again, that I was ready to embrace lesson 94 in which she wrote, "True light is strength. And strength is sinlessness. If you remain as God created you, you must be strong, and light must be in you. He who ensured your sinlessness must be the guarantee of strength and light as well. You are as God created you. Darkness cannot obscure the glory of God's Son. You stand in light, strong in the sinlessness in which you were created and in which you will remain throughout eternity."

It was my mama that said, *you'll understand it better by and by.* No, God is not done with me yet. But I have all that God gave me inside of me. I have begun to recognize and understand. No, not my understanding. I will *lean not into thine own understanding.* That lets me know that I must rely on the understanding of my relationship with God and on the wisdom of God. But it is me that holds the power to trust and have faith in God. I want this for you too.

People come into your life for a reason and a season. These women that I write about in this book represent various seasons of my life. Some are part of my entire life. They all brought me lessons. I do not see those lessons as harmful.

I guess I understand by and by!

Yes, there are people and principles of darkness that come to harm you, but I choose not to give that energy any light in this first book.

My Daddy once told me, "People can't hurt you unless you permit them to." Now that was hard to digest. He meant that people can't hurt you down in your soul unless you let them get down in there. People can also be a blessing to you, or you can let them destroy you. I chose to learn the lessons and receive the blessings.

I know God is in control of our faculties. Daddy also told me that people can affect you if you digest something from them that is not natural. I asked myself, how can I digest something that people give me? Things can be digested in many ways. My first thought was physical digestion. Later I realized you can digest things in many forms. You can eat it, hear it, think it and wear it. I will leave that there and save it for further explanation in the next book.

I have heard a few good Black women talk about the pain they felt due to their sons marrying White women. Some Black women believe that if their son marries a non-Black woman it means they don't love their mothers. I respectfully disagree with that sentiment. My son fell in love with a woman who is not

Black. And I know that my son loves me. And though he honors and celebrates my Blackness, he loves me because I raised him with love and nurtured him with my being. I taught him about love.

I remember a dark place in my life that caused me tremendous pain. It happened so fast. I didn't have time to question how I got there. The first person that came to mind when I was going through that period was my great grandmama. I cried out and believe it was her Spirit that came to remind me that I was from strong, mystical, powerful women. I needed to take the lessons I learned and the dreams I had and love on myself. I needed to be careful not to make choices that would get me in those dark places again. But if I ever found myself there, I have to recognize and understand that God and my ancestral mothers are with me. They come to remind me to trust God and have faith that I will get back to the light.

I'm getting older and the cost of getting older is you are forced to grow. I tell my daughter all the time. "Listen and heed the lessons now". You don't want to be 50 years old and just getting it. I am talking about understanding the by and by. I tell her to be in the moment and get it now.

I write about the women who have gone before me and some are a part of my journey now. I have only wet the mouthpiece of this writing instrument. There is so much more to my story, our story and how they are the tread and the breadcrumbs God weaved into my life. I can recall these moments in time and see myself in the reflection of the women who came to teach me.

I could not write about all the women that have touched me. It would take another lifetime to complete their stories. For now, I just want you to see the slivers of light in my path. I am who I am partly because of them.

I don't think some of the people who came on my path were just a coincidence. I think they were placed there for a reason. It was time for me to experience and learn the lesson I needed to learn to help me on my Journey.

I was listening to a YouTube video presentation by Howard Thurman my friend sent me the link to. In this video, Thurman asks the question, what is it that you really want? I realized my answer has always been the same. What I really want and have always wanted is to inspire someone. I have learned to seek that inspiration and inspire myself. I inspire myself to appreciate who I am and to affirm all the people I came from. Then I can inspire others.

All the lessons that helped shape me are a reflection of God's Holy Spirit that dwells in me. I was taught to recognize, praise and honor the Spirit of the Living God. By doing this, I get clear on how God wants to use me. I want to help heal and inspire people. I want everyone to experience the goodness of life. So, I share the stories where I got my inspiration from.

I encourage those around me to be yourself, love yourself and love one another. Find the traits in the Women that God placed in your life that was meant to show you to be you. Also, to love God with all your heart and soul. I know that sometimes I will doubt, I will fall short by making mistakes but making mistakes is part of being human. I want to be truly helpful and really be who God created. My great-grandmama told me in a dream once, "It's all about creativity." Therefore. I use my creativity to do the work God brought me here to do.

There are many signs and wonders God gave me to learn and become the woman He wants me to be.

He used angels, books, friends, encounters with acquaintances. He used my editor. I was afraid but my editor wouldn't entertain any conversations of doubt or lack. She clearly didn't want to hear it. She only wanted to see the next chapter. I kept writing and kept it moving. During our editing sessions, I heard my voice get stronger each time through her voice. For that I am grateful.

I want to inspire people with this book about my tiny experience with the people who inspired me. In addition, I want to leave a legacy of inspiration. I want my children and my grandchildren to know that we are standing on the shoulders of our ancestors. We are living in health and abundance in every area of our life because of the prayers that our ancestors spoke for us.

I recall all the songs from my childhood church. These songs often get me through the day. Songs like the hymnal, I Will Trust in the Lord.

"I will trust in the lord, I will trust In the Lord, I will trust in the Lord until I die".

I gave myself a life-changing gift of listening to the Holy Spirit. It was during my early twenties. I was distraught and in grief over the death of my brother. I did not know how to handle the inner turmoil I felt. I took to my bed. I cried and cried. It was a rainy day in Florida when I went to my childhood room that had a window looking out onto my neighbor's porch. A cool breeze blew through the window. I heard a still small voice. It said, "Trust me." It was a communication that I can't explain. I heard it in my ear, head, heart and soul. Trust me, the voice said again. I know now that this was the voice of the by and by. I also know that God wants me to trust Him however He shows up. I will continue to embrace the presence of God that I meet in every person.

During my 48th birthday year, I planned a pilgrimage with the intention of healing. I outlined and scheduled a trip back to the point when I first left home for college. I invited my daughter to fly in to share some of this with me. Just the first part. The college years. Mama said, you'll understand it by and by. I share this part of my journey with my daughter through this book. I had never backtracked. It was amazing.

I went to the campus. The bus ride along Peachtree Street that led me to the layout of the city. A city where I lived and worked to rediscover myself and grow. I went to the grave site of my brother's death. My brother that died in a car accident during my sophomore year in college. I included that in the pilgrimage because I knew that was the time I was stopped dead in my tracks. I was so devastated to have experienced the death of a loved one so suddenly.

I was told by a male friend once, "Until you come to terms with death, you will not fully enjoy life." I had always been afraid of death and especially of losing a loved one. It felt like abandonment. I let that grief stifle me. It truly interrupted my life for many years. It was a shocking experience and scared the life out of me. I am bravely now looking at the subject of my eternity.

I visited the location of the accident on Interstate 75. Just outside of Valdosta Georgia, just past the Hylea exit near the 2nd guard railing. Mama even remembered when the highway workers exchanged the railing for a new one years later. My mama made sure to remind us every year of that time and location. She mourned him forever.

I understand it in the by and by. I stop there and received a most profound blessing. I also visited his gravesite like never before. I was afraid to visit him before I did my healing work. After I was healed, I went into the cemetery alone for the first time. I stood by his gravesite and experienced so much peace and serenity. I accented the passage with so many rituals. I was truly blessed by the experience. Special thanks to my husband for joining me on the last leg of the trip which was outstanding.

This might sound crazy but afterwards, I wanted to run down the beach at night naked. I did, only I kept my twirling skirt on. I felt liberated.

Me and the Spirit,

216

Closely related, moving with the wind
Moving in time, always there
Ever present within
*Me, created in an image by God…..**thelma craig***

Chapter 35
After Thoughts

I wanted to write about all the woman that touched and impacted my life. They know who they are. But I was not able to write about Gladys, Regina, Adrianna, Shanda, Sharon, Loretta, Ellen, Peggy D, Mari B, Tracy, Carole, Shacoma (Pookie), Carolyn, Beverly, Lerita, and so on. As I was writing this book, so many came to mind, but I had to complete this task. It was for my healing. You all will be forever in my heart. I want all of them to know that I am grateful. And I see you. You continue to light up my path.

I read a quote by Matt McHargue recently. It said, "People grow when they are loved well. If you want to help someone heal, love them with an agenda." My life is about God's Agenda. And I know there is more to come. I can only hope I take all the lessons into my new life.

I could not finish this book without talking about all the people who helped me heal. Most of us have had traumatic experiences and encountered Satan himself in our lives. Some of those instances could have broken us--maybe a breaking was needed. But not all experiences were meant to break us. I submit, that when we embrace the experiences and the angels that we encounter, we can discover the blessings therein.

I could go on and on about who I met and who still shows up to represent for my good and growth. But I want to propose that we take the beautiful people and experiences that we encounter into account. That we recognize the women that have helped us be better people.

I really wanted to add a few good men to the list. Men like my brother, my Daddy, my son and my husband.

But when I mentioned the idea to my daughter and she said, "No. You can write another book about the men, another time." Needless to say, I wanted share with you how my brother taught me how to stand up and fight for myself. When the bullies wanted to fight me in elementary school. my brother made me fight back. He said he was tired of me not being my best. I had it in me. He brought it out.

He said, "They will continue to affect you in your ear if you don't stop it."

He also said that if I didn't fight this one girl, that he would fight me. He would fight me until I fought back. I fought the bully and won.

I also wanted to write a little bit about my Daddy. I wanted to tell you how he made me feel safe, loved and beautiful. When I was little, he always rescued me when the world was closing in, calling me Black and ugly. He let me know that I was Black and beautiful. He had a nickname for me that only he could call me and he passionately pronounced it loudly. And I'm proud to share it now. He called me, "Black Gal" until the day he died. And that day was truly a blessing. I was there with him holding his hand and reading a prayer from the Bible. The 23rd Psalm. Another great opportunity to stand in the gap for my parents on their deathbed. Another chance to make a transition tranquil. To ispire.

It would have been nice to tell you a little something about my son. My son reminds me of my brother. He is smart, tough and kind. My son shows me every day the attributes I so love and cherished in my Daddy, my father-in-law, my brother and my husband. They are and were great loving men. He is just carrying out their legacy. I am so proud to see that.

Oh, and I would've written about my husband who has been has been my rock through it all. He was my friend at first. I didn't want to marry my friend. But I knew it was the right thing. Because our friendship is what keeps us together when times are tough. He doesn't talk much—that's because I do. He doesn't mind that about me. But when he tells me something that my souls urge me to do, I listen. He was another to tell me that when I find a friend, I am truly blessed.

I found myself in the midst of healing when I wrote about the women that God placed in my life. This was my time with God. This is what I want for you. I want you to recall and remember all the things women have taught you. It's about creativity in everything you do. The most intense experiences, relationships and interactions with the people in our life are not just happenstance. I believe that God places them in our life for purposeful reasons. It is essential that we look back on our life to the path that the breadcrumbs have laid out.

As I get older God provides loaves of bread. Powerful revelations about who I am and how to be. The women that impacted my life did so in such a way that I am still celebrating the outcome.

Don't get me wrong, I couldn't share every single experience that I recall. I am shivering at a glimpse of what God can do. And if we listen and take heed, even after the hardest experiences, we will see that God has a great plan.

One of my favorite scriptures come to mind when I reminisce on the people and experiences God has granted me. I may not have recognized the blessing at the time, but I absolutely know that God was at work. I am still in the recalling process.

"I praise you because I am fearfully and wonderfully made. Your works are wonderful. I know that full well. Psalms 139:14 NIV

I recently read a quote on a site that I follow on *Facebook* called *Wild Woman Sisterhood.* It said, "You can tell who the strong women are. They are the ones you see building each other up instead of tearing each other down."

The women in this book were there to build me up even though I or they already knew God's purpose for me. I was not fully aware of their purpose in my life at the time, but I am now.

I also read something the other day that resonated with me. It said, "Since the very beginning you and I should have been learning from our life's events. Now we have the luxury of examining our life in reflection of where we've been and who we are."

This is our journey, our life. This is the by and by my mama was talking about.

I am a grown woman now. I have the sense and spirit enough to know that in the Lord's prayer – Matthew said, "Lead me in the path of righteousness for His namesake. Yea, though I walk through the valley of the shadow of death, I will fear no evil." For me, this means that because they were and are with me, God is with me." He sent his agents and angels to teach me and hold me up. I get some of it now. If I got all of it, I don't think I could handle it. The people God put in my path were to teach me and touch me in ways that will allow me to see the light that is inside me.

I was once told by a male friend, "Your light shines too bright." How can a light shine too bright? It's the light from God, it's the light from my mama's laughter with that sassy sense of humor and outstanding sense of fashion. It's my Mama's faith. It's my great grandmama's twinkle in her eye, her prophesy and dreams. It's Miss Susie's elusive and mystical nature and Miss Rollins high, proper and mighty way she carried herself.

When the light is shining through me, I can see it. I can remember them. And those are great lessons. They are a great light to shine on my path.

Chaka Chan's song goes," *I'm every woman, its all in me"*

. By and By, I see. I see your light. I know how it got there. I know you. I know and love myself. I love God and am so grateful for the relationship. To all my readers I say, LOVE GOD AS HE CREATED YOU.

Remember the gifts and people he presented to you. Be the great woman you meant to be. That will take some reflection and trust. I am giving you some tools from this book to help you do just that.

1) Sit and reminisce about the woman or sisters, mothers, aunts, cousins or daughters that impacted your life.

2) Write about an experience that comes to mind about these persons.

3) Ask yourself what the lesson is?

4) Compile the memories.

5) Most importantly, embrace the experiences and share the wisdom with other women and girls who are healing.

Blessed be, the waves that spread on the beach
Bring pebbles, shells and rocks on the shore
On the water, amidst the moon's glistening light
To beautify, edify and glorify….thelma craig

Great Grandma Always Said...........,

"Fool. Don't you Know the Blacker the Berry the sweeter the juice" Hold yo head up and love the color God gave you! (A quote from unknown)

"You got to Let that shit go"

"I pray all de time for my chillen and my grandchillen"

" I'm Sitting here waiting for the Lord to carry me home" (In her last years after she hi100 years)

"Watch out for dem foolish eyes"

"Waiting for de Lord to come carry me home"

Mama Always Said…………

"God may not come when you want him to, But he will surely come on time"

" You are gonna have to give account to God for that action"

"God will make a way out of no way"

"God won't give you more that you can handle"

"I'm just gonna hold onto God's unchanging hand"

"Father I stretch my hands to thee, for no other help know" (when eve she was in a stressful situation)

"Mark my words…

"Please don't wear those shite shoes after Labor Day"

You got more sense than I thought" (laughing lovingly after you surprise her with accomplishment)

"Listen to that ole Song, God Specializes"

They will need me before I need You.

That ain't nothing but the devil (when she found herself in chaos)

"Take it to the Lord n Prayer"

(*NOTE: These quotes are not their originals; Just noting some quotes I recall hearing them say from time to time. You will find a blessing if you will recall some of your Moms Saying's; we keep them alive in our hearts)

Quotes from others

"The Butterfly does not look back at the caterpillar in same, just as you should not look back at your past in shame. Your past was part of your own transformation"-----unknown

"If You want to Fly, You have to give up the things that weigh you down
-----Toni Morrison

"There is no time for despair, no place for self-pity, no need for silence, no room for fear. We speak, we write, we do language. That is how civilizations heal"
----Toni Morrison

"One of the hardest things in life to learn are which bridges to cross and which bridges to burn."
— Oprah Winfrey

"Surround yourself only with people who are going to take you higher."
— Oprah Winfrey

"Turn your wounds into wisdom."
---- Oprah Winfrey

"When you don't show up as who you are, people fall in love with who you're not. Then when they find out who you are, that's when they leave."
----Iyanla Vanzant

Blank Page Note Page- recall your favorites quotes

Made in the USA
Columbia, SC
11 March 2020